RETHINKING
SCHOOL
INSPECTION

IS THERE A BETTER WAY?

TRACEY O'BRIEN

JOHN CATT

FROM HODDER EDUCATION

First published 2023

by John Catt Educational Ltd,
15 Riduna Park, Station Road,
Melton, Woodbridge IP12 1QT

Tel: +44 (0) 1394 389850
Email: enquiries@johncatt.com
Website: www.johncatt.com

ISBN: 978 1 3983 8746 1

Set and designed by John Catt Educational Limited

CONTENTS

FOREWORD

How can you accurately judge any school in two days?

School leader

Midway through writing this book, I got 'the call'. I've had the call before, but this time felt different, as I was acutely aware of how I was beginning to feel about the current inspection model. I had been pulling together my thoughts based on my experiences and those of others, and had conducted research into accountability models in other sectors and other nations. I had interviewed people who had written inspection frameworks and leaders who had been through different ones. Now here I was, my own living case study. There was a reason this inspection was so different. I am a secondary school leader, but while writing this book I was offered the opportunity to be the Headteacher of a primary school. I felt this would be a brilliant experience; it would help me understand inspection more broadly across different phases, and I would learn a lot. The school was a 'non-association independent school' – I hadn't heard of that – and the inspection handbook, while similar to the usual one, was different. The inspection would be carried out using the Independent School Standards – of which I had no experience – as well as those of Ofsted. So, on my eighth day in post, I answered the phone...

Well, I learned a lot in a very short time. The principles are the same: how well do you know the school? What are its strengths and weaknesses? What are you doing to address the latter? The school was very small and I became increasingly aware of the many hats each of us wore as staff members and how the level of 'interrogation' was at times seemingly overwhelming. You only do really appreciate other people's experiences when you live through them, and I clearly saw that the process of inspection is no different in a small setting than in a large secondary school, and that in some cases it may even be harder as there is so much focus on a relatively small group of people.

In the afternoon of the final day of the inspection I picked up a copy of *Headteacher Update* and put it in my bag. When I got home I opened it and saw 12 pages dedicated to Ofsted preparation!

The dilemma is this: Ofsted is often seen as good or outstanding by people who get good or outstanding in their school inspection, and Ofsted is often seen as inadequate for people who don't. It is of course not as straightforward as this. Many leaders and school staff don't feel happy with Ofsted, either the institution, the framework, or the process. This can be true even if they get one of the two 'top' grades. Some who do well with the grade judgement may feel the experience has been an overly bureaucratic and exhausting process and might think it could be refined or adapted in some way. Some school leaders who get 'downgraded', though disappointed, may actually feel the process and outcome was fair. I call this the Ofsted Paradox.

The number of comments I read about Ofsted on social media, in educational magazines and in news articles is increasing exponentially. Surely this is telling us something, especially when the vast majority of comments are negative in some way. I've read and heard that 'Ofsted is broken', and 'our accountability system is broken'. Most educators and stakeholders would agree we need some form of accountability in our schools, and while there is some common discourse about an 'other way', we are not in agreement just yet. Some of the unions have made useful comments and there has been a lot written about what Ofsted should not be. But what could it be?

We are a public sector profession using public money to serve the nation's children, families and communities. In my last book, *School self-review – a sensible approach*, I wrote about the purpose of accountability in English schools.[1] I stated that it is of course right that we are held to account: we operate in the public sector, we are responsible for the education

---

1   O'Brien, T. (2022) *School self-review – a sensible approach*. Woodbridge: John Catt.

and prospects of young people, and we spend public money. We must demonstrate that we are worthy of the trust we are given and the resources allocated to us. I also suggested that my ideal accountability model would be one where we are trusted as professionals to carry out our own internal self-evaluation and peer review practices, with these then being validated by an external body such as Ofsted.

So is there a better way? A way that more people in education will feel they can support?

We hear that inspection regimes are different in other countries, but are they? What about accountability frameworks in other public services in the UK? What can we learn from being more outward looking?

This book aims to reflect on these issues and offer some suggestions as to how schools should or could be held to account in this country. It examines what a meaningful accountability system of school inspection could look like, and I hope it leads to some fruitful discussions. There may be a few disagreements but hopefully it might be agreed that as a body of professionals some account might be taken of what we feel is best for ourselves and the children in our care.

I recognise that Ofsted is not just applicable to state schools, but this book solely relates to the school inspection arm of their work. It is not strictly an academic work, rather it draws on the wide range of views and opinions available about the current state of inspection in this country, and the gathering and growing volume of voices from different quarters that are dissatisfied with Ofsted and the intense 'make or break' pressures it involves. I could have spent more time looking at academic research (though as we will see there isn't much out there about the impact of Ofsted), but there is a pressing need to address the issues involved, and I don't believe we can wait any longer to implement substantive and lasting change.

CHAPTER 1
WHAT IS WRONG WITH OUR CURRENT SCHOOL INSPECTION MODEL?

Our annual survey of over 3,082 education staff found that in 2022 record numbers of UK teachers and education staff have considered leaving the sector in the past academic year due to pressures on their mental health and wellbeing. Over half of staff have actively sought to change or leave their current jobs, citing workload as the main factor.

Teacher Wellbeing Index 2022[2]

The *Teacher Wellbeing Index* report highlights many of the issues causing stress and anxiety in schools and analyses the key underlying factors behind them. One area explored was workplace culture, where the report notes that, 'positive organisational culture, good quality support for staff and trusting line management relationships are linked with better individual wellbeing. This is especially important to recognise right now. The current context – of financial and staffing challenges, Government and policy instability, as well as pressure from Ofsted – makes the creation

---

2   Education Support (2023) *Teacher Wellbeing Index*. Available at: https://www. educationsupport.org.uk/resources/for-organisations/research/teacher-wellbeing-index/?utm_source=Twitter+&utm_medium=social+&utm_campaign=twix22

of positive, productive and psychologically safe cultures incredibly challenging.' Some of these things cannot be controlled by the individual school, such as funding levels and the state of our economy, but we should, as leaders, be able to influence our own policy makers with our thoughts about school inspection. The continuing call that inspections are stressful and overly bureaucratic continues to rise in volume.

The findings of the *Teacher Wellbeing Index* report were supported by those in the report *Pressures on Middle Leaders in Schools.*[3] Some of the comments around views of Ofsted and inspection collected in this report highlighted that, 'In particular, subject-leads were quick to reference the threat of Ofsted deep-dives as a major source of anxiety.' It is clear that the participants in this study feel there is a 'discrepancy in Ofsted's stated aim to reduce teacher workloads versus heightened expectations during inspections':

> *I think the drive from Ofsted now in terms of the expectation of people to know a subject inside out, is new and putting pressure on teachers.*
>
> Subject lead at a primary school

> *There seems to be a big mismatch in some of the big things Ofsted want. They really want teachers' workloads to be reduced, but at the same time … the expectations around subject leadership are much more intense than they were three, four years ago.*
>
> EYFS lead at a primary school

Mary Bousted's 2022 book *Support not Surveillance* highlights the issue of teachers leaving the profession 'increasingly early in their careers' and reflects that the DfE 2020 census shows that of those entering the profession in 2011, over one fifth left within their first three years, increasing to over a quarter for the 2016 cohort. One of the reasons cited for this comes from a DfE paper in 2017 showing that among such issues as workload and feeling undervalued, Ofsted pressure was a key factor. She writes that 'school leaders' fear of Ofsted contributes to their undervaluing of teachers'

---

3   Education Support (2022) *Pressures on Middle Leaders in Schools.* Available at: https://www.educationsupport.org.uk/media/uenogeia/pressure-on-middle-leaders.pdf

knowledge and professional experience, which leaves teachers detached from decisions about curriculum, teaching and learning strategies and assessment'. She also quotes Chris Woodhead (Chief HMI 1994-2000) when he said he wanted 'Ofsted to be a weapon of fear'. It is not surprising that this wish has been realised for so many.

Tom Sherrington's view that 'I've also made the case time and time again that our current accountability culture is excessive with very significant negative consequences for schools, leaders, teachers, children, and by association, parents – and the country as a whole' is shared by many.[4] Sherrington shares his thoughts around the current inspection model. He writes that school inspection is a 'key stick element' that drives school behaviours by force of the risk or threat of negative consequences. Figure 1 demonstrates this thinking.[5]

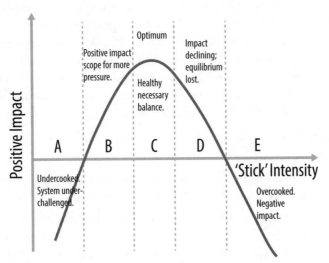

Figure 1. Sherrington's accountability 'stick'

4   Sherrington, T. (2023) 'Ofsted "Inadequate" – the emblem of our toxic system.' *teacherhead.* Available at: https://teacherhead.com/2019/05/05/ofsted-inadequate-the-emblem-of-our-toxic-system/

5   Sherrington, T. (2017) 'Accountability "stick" is taking us to the brink: Time for radical change.' *teacherhead.* Available at: https://teacherhead.com/2017/12/13/accountability-stick-is-taking-us-to-the-brink-time-for-radical-change/

He writes that in zone A with little accountability the system is underchallenged and so schools don't move forward. In zone B, the accountability pressure is beginning to be just right, enabling schools to 'implement positive sustainable change'. Sherrington calls zone C the 'sweet spot', where the pressure put on schools by inspection is at its optimum. However, after that, things go downhill. In zone D he suggests, 'positive gains are diminished by negative effects: teachers start leaving; school cultures become toxic, perverse incentives start taking effect over principled decisions.' He suggests we are now in zone E where 'the stick intensity is so high that teacher recruitment and retention become unsustainably low, too many schools are patching things together, leadership turnover is unsustainably high, the quality, breadth and depth of curriculum is damaged by short-term outcomes-driven practices'.

Sherrington's call for action is that, 'unless we recognise that and dial down the counterproductive intensity with some urgency we're going to fall over the edge. Instead of recruiting teachers and leaders into a system where we've all got guns to our heads, we need to create a professional culture where the challenges schools face are seen as shared problems, where the solutions are not about blame and vilification and where officials and politicians drop all the "tough talk". It has to stop.'

The report 'Does Ofsted need improvement?' in *The Week*[6] reveals the following:

- Fewer than one in ten teachers think Ofsted has raised standards at their school, according to polling for *The Times*.

- A survey of 5,000 teachers found 'overwhelming levels of unhappiness' with the government watchdog, as the vast majority of teachers told pollsters they would rate the regulator as 'inadequate' or 'requires improvement'.

- Just 0.5% of teachers polled by the Times Education Commission said Ofsted's performance was outstanding, and only 13% said it was good.

---

6   The Week (2022) 'Does Ofsted Require Improvement?' *The Week*. 14 June. Available at: https://www.theweek.co.uk/news/education/957060/does-ofsted-require-improvement

- Respondents were also asked whether Ofsted had improved education at their school: 59% disagreed.

- The commission said that its final report showed there has been a 'breakdown of trust' between Ofsted and schools, and will recommend reforms so that the watchdog works more collaboratively with headteachers.

- Headteachers have said that the 'intense pressure' of Ofsted inspections means that school staff are resigning from the profession.

These findings demonstrate what many believe is wrong with our current school inspection regime. It's not hard to find criticism in the press and on social media, and we do need to be open minded about the benefits an inspectorate can bring in terms of assuring quality and holding schools to account, but there seems to be so much unhappiness out there right now.

In a blog on the NEU site[7] Frank Coffield, Emeritus Professor of Education at UCL Institute of Education, examines the some of the issues in greater depth:

- The problems of teacher recruitment and retention have intensified. Part of the reason is that too many senior staff, anxious to hold on to their own jobs, now behave as if they were Ofsted inspectors who create in their schools regimes of 'hyper-accountability.'

- Able teachers, repeatedly assessed as 'outstanding', still have their preparation, teaching, management of behaviour and marking of students' work evaluated incessantly. The pressures created by Ofsted cascade down through the system increasing teachers' stress and workloads to the point of exhaustion and burn-out.

- Overall Ofsted's methods are unreliable, invalid, ineffective and unjust, especially to schools serving the poorest communities. Most teachers view it, not as a useful lever for change, but as a hammer that creates a climate of fear and intimidation. Ofsted has failed to balance challenge with an equal concern for support.

---

7   Coffield, F. (2022) *Ofsted still causes more harm than good.* National Education Union. Available at: https://neu.org.uk/blog/ofsted-still-causes-more-harm-good

Recurring themes of anxiety, workload pressures, stress, and consequences for the recruitment and retention of teachers abound, as well as the question of whether Ofsted actually works in terms of school improvement and raising standards. Like others, I have turned to Twitter. Not to vent or whinge but to take a snapshot of feelings towards our inspection regime. I am well aware that there are caveats around such an activity: who goes on twitter, who might want to respond, who is on my feed and so on, but it is a weathervane of sorts. I posed a question back in Autumn 2022, quite open, and asked for answers to be kept short and clean. My question was:

'When I say Ofsted, you say ... (one word answers, no swearing, and I am genuinely looking for a balanced view please!)'

Responses came in quickly and I did not keep it going for long: as I said, I wanted a quick bit of feedback. I've put the responses in a word cloud (figure 2), and as you can see they weren't all negative. However, out of over 100 responses, some messages were clear. The strongest message was that people thought of Ofsted as inconsistent. Many shared conversations related to the inspection team itself. There were concerns about whether staff trusted the team, their experience and their ability to really listen. Some wondered if inspectors had hidden agendas or if some were using the 'secret crib sheets' some of us have seen. Several Twitter respondents said Ofsted was outdated or stressful.

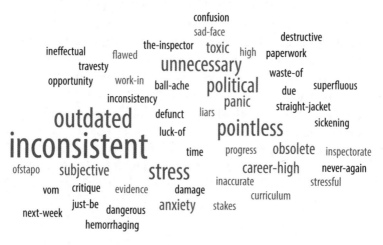

Figure 2. Quick Twitter survey about thoughts on Ofsted

All these issues will be explored in greater detail later in the book when we look at some real case studies of people's experiences of inspection or their fear of it.

Some respondents didn't stick to the task and wrote more than one word. A few of my favourites towards the end of the survey included:

- Judging by the response (on here) if Ofsted wanted a positive relationship with schools they are failing and doing more harm than good.
- Can I ask a question? Please complete the sentence – What Ofsted did for me?
- I once ate 5 slices of cake in one day during an Ofsted inspection. I'm not proud of it. I stress eat. That's a lot of stress. But seriously. Why don't they inspect CPD and demand certain standards?
- Sadly I mostly agree (with the comments). Wouldn't it be great if everyone described them as 'useful'.

Two people commented that it was a career high, and I think this is where one of the greatest concerns lies. It can be a career high: taking a school from one judgement to another is rewarding and satisfying, a relief, and it validates everyone's efforts. However, for many headteachers, validation from a two-day visit from a handful of people doesn't begin to reflect their years of hard work, sweat and often tears. In my last book I wrote about how an inspector said she would 'believe' my judgement of the quality of teaching and learning in the school based on my observation of a single maths lesson that we would observe together. Such methodologies would be laughable if it weren't for the fact that the reputations of so many individuals and institutions are at stake.

I knew that people were looking at how AI is quick at drawing on a general consensus of material for its results, so I asked Chat GPT if Ofsted was effective. It said, 'Ofsted has been effective in identifying areas for improvement in schools and encouraging schools to make changes. However, there is ongoing debate about the effectiveness of Ofsted inspections in improving educational outcomes. Some argue that the focus on exam results and data can lead to a narrow curriculum and teaching to the test, while others believe that the accountability provided by Ofsted is necessary to ensure that schools are meeting their responsibilities to students.' This also demonstrates that the debate is live and ongoing and must be addressed immediately.

In November 2021 The DfE published *The Education Staff Wellbeing Charter.*[8] The then Education Minister Nadhim Zahawi wrote: 'This charter sets out commitments from this department, from Ofsted and employers working in education on actions to protect and promote the wellbeing of education staff.' In the charter Ofsted recognised that 'staff can feel that inspections are a source of stress' and made certain commitments:

1. We will ensure that inspectors take staff wellbeing into account in coming to their judgements and monitor this through quality assurance and evaluation.

2. We will review whether the framework is having inadvertent impacts on staff wellbeing (for example, creating unnecessary workload) and take steps to alleviate any issues.

3. We will continue to clarify that we do not expect providers to create documentation for inspection, to try to reduce administrative workload.

I think we would all agree with Ofsted looking into these potential issues and would welcome as much alleviation of stress as possible. However, I would argue that there is much, much more that we need to evaluate, review and change about our current inspection model than the issues mentioned above.

Writing for *Schools Week*[9] Kathryn Snowdon listed Ofsted stress as the first point in her response to the Ofsted report *Teacher well-being at work in schools and further education providers.*[10] She commented that teachers

8   Department for Education (2021) *The Education Staff Wellbeing Charter.* Available at: https://assets.publishing.service.gov.uk/government/uploads/system/uploads/attachment_data/file/1034032/DfE_Education_Workforce_Welbeing_Charter_Nov21.pdf

9   Snowdon, K. (2019) Inspections cause teacher stress, and 4 other findings from Ofsted's wellbeing research. *Schools Week.* 22 July. Available at: https://schoolsweek.co.uk/ofsted-teacher-well-being-report-key-findings/

10   Ofsted (2019) *Teacher well-being at work in schools and further education providers.* Available at: https://assets.publishing.service.gov.uk/government/uploads/system/uploads/attachment_data/file/936253/Teacher_well-being_report_110719F.pdf

can fear Ofsted inspections, that they felt there was additional workload before inspections and that this created longer working hours. She writes, 'there were also calls for Ofsted to be a less "threatening" organisation. Inspectors should instead be able to build professional, constructive and "formative" relationships with school staff.' Many teachers, leaders and governors would agree, I am sure, that this last point about formative relationships is key if Ofsted and the current system of inspection is to lead to school improvement.

Ofsted itself comments regarding its own inspections: 'Educators also feel that Ofsted inspections are a source of stress – this is largely because inspections are reported to increase administrative workload (though part of this appears to be driven by senior leadership) or because there is an excessive focus on data/exam results, which narrows educators' focus to test outcomes rather than quality education.'[11] What I find interesting here, and this is supported by comments in the report, is that teachers feel that inspection stress cascades down through the school, from senior leaders to staff. There is no doubt this happens in very many cases, often unintentionally, but the level of quality assurance, Ofsted interview practice, deep dives, triangulation and form filling that middle leaders end up having to do causes huge workload. Ofsted will say they don't ask for this to be done, but if we consider the high stakes nature of inspection, it is not a surprise that Trust leaders and headteachers 'make' this happen.

One of Ofsted's own recommendations in their report is that leaders should:

> *Familiarise yourselves and your staff with the new education inspection framework (EIF) to avoid unnecessary workload.Educators told us that they experienced high levels of workload through collecting data for Ofsted, and that our frameworks had led to too much emphasis on attainment. The EIF re-focuses inspection on quality of education with the curriculum at its heart. Unnecessary data should not be collected for inspection.*[11]

The shift in the framework from outcomes to curriculum was welcomed by many, but had enormous unintended consequences for middle leaders all over the country who had to write lengthy documents about

---

11   Ibid.

curriculum intent and implementation. It's not that this focused thinking around curriculum design and decisions is unwelcome, but that the level of document production required to prove these conversations have happened has been quite extraordinary. It is no wonder that many teachers and leaders are turning to 'off the shelf' curricula where this work has already been done and written up.

We need to work out a way forward which enables us to demonstrate we know our schools without generating an unnecessary workload, and which reduces the burden of accountability we feel in schools. Ofsted state that an 'Evaluation of the implementation of the EIF will look at the extent to which the framework is leading to unnecessary workload, so that steps can be taken to alleviate any issues' and I am sure we look forward to their findings and recommendations.

Claudia Civinini wrote that, 'analysing data from the 2018 Teaching and Learning International Survey (Talis), researchers found that more than two-thirds (68 per cent) of teachers in England reported feeling accountability-related stress compared with less than half (45 per cent) of teachers globally.'[12] She comments on the remarks of one of the researchers, Professor John Jerrim, who states: 'We also believe that our findings highlight the need for policymakers to recognise that increasing accountability within the school system is unlikely to be a one-way street to "school improvement".' He adds: 'Accountability is becoming increasingly common within school systems across the world, yet many are concerned about the impact it is having upon teachers' workload and wellbeing and whether this is turning people away from the teaching profession.'

A 2021 article written in FE News[13] captures some views about Ofsted given in evidence to The Times Education Commission,[14] which includes some pretty damning messages:

---

12   Civinini, C. (2021) England a world leader in teacher stress. *TES*. 18 March. Available at: https://www.tes.com/magazine/news/general/england-world-leader-teacher-stress

13   FE News (2021) *Ofsted is a 'reign of terror', Dame Alison Peacock tells The Times Education Commission*. Available at: https://www.fenews.co.uk/skills/ofsted-is-a-reign-of-terror-dame-alison-peacock-tells-the-times-education-commission/

14   The Times Education Commission (2022) *The Times Education Commission Final Report*. Available at: https://s3.documentcloud.org/documents/22056664/times-education-commission-final-report.pdf

Ofsted, frankly, it's a reign of terror. They come in, they start to sort of talk in, kind of, highfalutin language about research outcomes and so on and curriculum coherence. It's designed to put people on the backfoot. The more that we can enable teachers to be research literate themselves, to be able to make decisions that are informed by evidence in their classroom, that they feel confident about, that they can see the impact of, they're more likely to be able to stand their ground and actually supersede whatever an inspection regime wants. That was my experience as a headteacher.

Dame Alison Peacock, CEO of the Chartered College of Teaching

I would get rid of Ofsted. You know, I'm happy for there to be an inspection system – of course there has to be accountability in the education system, of course there does. But, in my view, Ofsted has become a toxic brand, if you like. It's become synonymous with stress and, what's the word, sort of a punitive approach to inspection. I just feel that, you know, people talk about reform of Ofsted, I just feel it needs to be replaced with a different system and the stakes need to be lowered. People shouldn't be in fear that their jobs are at stake if a particular child doesn't get a particular result.

Ryan Wilson, author and former teacher

Ofsted's specific list is based on what you're doing wrong. It's not done as supportive or to help you improve. There's a threat of league tables and bad ratings that loom. And then, on the day, we used to kick out the naughty kids and tell them to stay at home or send them off on a trip. So, how is that in the interests of the child?

Mehreen Baig, presenter and former teacher

In 2018, the report of the NAHT Accountability Commission commented that despite wanting to create the greatest education system in the world, 'too many of the incentives and sanctions in our system are working against this ambition.'[15]

---

15 NAHT (2018) *Improving School Accountability. Report of the NAHT Accountability Commission*. Available at: https://www.naht.org.uk/Portals/0/PDF's/Improving%20 school%20accountability.pdf?ver=2021-04-27-121950-093/

To achieve greatness we need good people, in the right places, doing the right things, but the accountability system is failing on all three counts. It is driving good people out of the profession: directly, as the consequence of perceived drops in performance and indirectly, through the unmanageable workload associated with it and a pervasive culture of fear. It dissuades good teachers and leaders from working in challenging schools for fear of being treated unfairly by the inspectorate. … Perhaps most concerning of all, it has celebrated and encouraged defensive and insular leadership behaviours that, if unchecked, will limit our capacity to improve.

The report agrees that Ofsted identifies failure and that there should be no poor schools, but comments that, 'The accountability system provides little benefit to the pupils, parents and staff at the vast majority of schools in this country that are not failing,' adding that, 'the approaches used by the government to hold schools to account are acting as a brake to overall improvement and are, on balance, doing more harm than good.'

I feel that it would be a positive step if, as part of an Ofsted inspection or as part of the framework, credit were given to schools who were actually out there supporting other schools. This would negate some of the divisive and competitive outcomes of inspections. It could demonstrate that we are all working towards a self-improving system, especially in a time of such limited resources. We could revisit the notion of 'every school a good school'.

Of course, there is the ever-present question of whether we need inspections at all. On reading an Ofsted report about whether grades should be retained when making judgements about schools' overall effectiveness, I was intrigued by what I saw in figure 3. Is it a coincidence that schools' P8 scores match so closely with their Ofsted grades? Given the picture here I wonder if inspectors need to visit schools at all! Ofsted say they don't look at data but the correlation here is pretty obvious. Does the same correlation still pertain today?

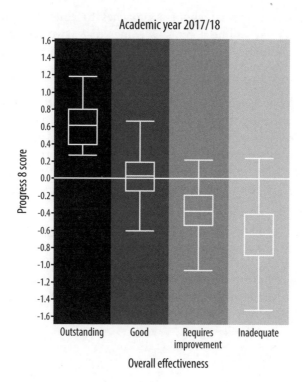

Figure 3. The relationship between Progress 8 scores and overall effectiveness grades[16]

Even some former inspectors agree that Ofsted, as it is, has become irrelevant. In a 2022 TES article they shared their views. They suggest, 'there comes a point when it is worth considering whether inspection is really adding value.' They add that, 'it is time to deploy an inspector of safeguarding on a fairly regular basis' as part of the role of the inspectorate. This is a suggestion I argue for in the conclusion of this book.

These comments are only a representative sample. Many school leaders are at breaking point, and many agree with some of the sentiments in this chapter. Some said the lockdowns gave us an amazing opportunity

---

16 Ofsted (2019) *Retaining the current grading system in education. Some arguments and evidence.* Available at: https://assets.publishing.service.gov.uk/government/uploads/system/uploads/attachment_data/file/936220/Retaining_the_current_grading_system_-_arguments_and_evidence_290419.pdf

for a rethink and a reset about approaches to education, and while some practices like online parents' evenings may have remained, other things like examinations and inspections have returned to pre-pandemic methods.

> *The pandemic appeared to provide a moment to rethink, to consider the function and purpose of institutions such as Ofsted in a context where it seemed teachers were revalued as integral to the wellbeing of the nation, and their professional judgement was to be trusted, particularly in terms of examination results. Ofsted suspended all inspections during the first full lockdown of 2020, and schools were, briefly, set free from the perceived need to be 'Ofsted-ready'.*
>
> Jane Perryman, Professor of Sociology of Education at
> UCL Institute of Education[17]

If we don't seize the moment for this rethink about school inspection now, then the next framework will come along, and then the next, by which time we will have very few teachers and even fewer leaders left in our institutions.

---

17   Perryman, J. (2022) Ofsted is more stick than carrot. Blog post. *NEU*. Available at: https://neu.org.uk/blog/ofsted-more-stick-carrot

CHAPTER 2
THE PURPOSE OF SCHOOL ACCOUNTABILITY AND INSPECTION

It is right that, as a publicly funded universal service, the education system should be subject to an appropriate, constructive and proportionate system of accountability.

NASUWT, 2017[18]

The NASUWT *School Accountability Position Statement* notes that, 'Across the UK, hierarchical accountability is the dominant form of school accountability. For example, governments/administrations use inspection, test and examination data, and in England, published performance tables to hold schools to account. The hierarchical approach that dominates external systems of accountability is often replicated through accountability systems that operate within individual schools, such as the performance management of teachers.'[19]

---

18   NASUWT (2023) *Inspection and Accountability.* Available at: https://www.nasuwt.org.uk/advice/in-the-classroom/inspection-and-accountability.html
19   NASUWT (2017) *School Accountability Position Statement.* Available at: https://www.nasuwt.org.uk/static/uploaded/8fb3ea40-12e5-49f2-a215735638746d8a.pdf

The NASUWT believe there are ten principles (figure 4) which should underpin our approach to accountability in schools. These ten principles will be referred to again in chapter 9 where we consider some alternatives to the current school inspection framework.

SYSTEMS OF SCHOOL ACCOUNTABILITY SHOULD:

1. Trust teachers as professionals.

2. Support schools to provide a curriculum that is broad, balanced and meets the needs of all learners.

3. Support schools to maintain high educational standards.

4. Support teachers and school leaders to improve the quality of teaching and learning.

5. Encourage and support teachers and school leaders to work co-operatively and collaboratively.

6. Be fair and equitable.

7. Ensure that teachers and school leaders are supported to engage in dialogue and collaborative decision-making.

8. Ensure that the needs and priorities of learners and parents are considered and taken into account appropriately in decision-making.

9. Be streamlined and avoid unnecessary bureaucracy and workload.

10. Be rigorous, reasonable and valid.

Figure 4. NASUWT principles to underpin our approach to accountability in schools

The NASUWT suggests that these principles, 'challenge the notion that school accountability should simply be hierarchical. They recognise that accountability may also be "professional", peer-to-peer and bottom up.' This is a recurring theme and one which has growing support.

In May 2018, the Department for Education produced a document called *Principles for a clear and simple accountability system*.[20] They stated that 'Accountability is a key component of our school system' and that, 'Accountability matters – every child deserves a great education. We have a responsibility to ensure all pupils are getting a great education, and we will be unapologetic in acting where pupils' education is suffering.' Can we argue with this? We all want our children to be taught by the best practitioners and support staff in the best schools, and we need systems in place to ensure everyone who attends school is safe.

In my book *School self-review – a sensible approach*, I wrote 'it is of course right that we are held to account: we operate in the public sector, we are responsible for the education and prospects of young people, and we spend public money. We must demonstrate that we are worthy of the trust and resources allocated to us', and this remains true.[21] I referenced the work of Chapman and Sammons and have been drawn back to a distinction they proposed between school effectiveness and school improvement. When we look at figure 5 it seems that the purpose of Ofsted is to look at effectiveness and not improvement. This is very interesting and maybe we could consider this in greater depth. If we have top down accountability then what should it be for? Should it be to say 'this school is effective (or not)', and focus on the left side of the table? Should we then take away the mantra that Ofsted 'improves schools', with the right-hand side of the column being left to the schools and the school system itself?

---

20 DfE (2018) *Principles for a clear and simple accountability system*. Available at: https://assets.publishing.service.gov.uk/government/uploads/system/uploads/attachment_data/file/704865/Principles_for_a_clear_and_simple_accountability_system.pdf

21 O'Brien, T. (2022) *School self-review – a sensible approach*. Woodbridge: John Catt.

	School effectiveness	School improvement
1.	Focus on schools	Focus on teachers
2.	Focus on organisation	Focus on school processes
3.	Data-driven, emphasis on outcomes	Empirical evaluation of the effects of changes
4.	Quantitative in orientation	Qualitative in orientation
5.	Lack of knowledge about how to implement change strategies	Exclusively concerned with change in schools
6.	More concerned with change in pupil outcomes	More concerned with journey of school improvement than its destination
7.	More concerned with schools at one point in time	More concerned with schools as changing
8.	Based on research knowledge	Focused on practitioner knowledge

Figure 5. The separate traditions of school effectiveness and school improvement[22]

In a blog about Ofsted, Paul Main states that, 'central to this important establishment is the welfare of some of our most vulnerable people. Without an organisation looking after us, any institution offering childcare or education could pretty much do what they wanted. Having an Inspectorate raises the standard across-the-board.'[23]

I agree with the importance of ensuring all our young people's needs are catered for, but I am not sure all school leaders would currently agree that our inspectorate raises standards across the board.

A 2018 report by the NFER defines accountability 'broadly as a government's mechanism for holding educational institutions to account for the delivery of high quality education.'[24] The accountability paradox is that on the one hand accountability can contribute to improvements

---

22 Chapman, C. and Sammons, P. (2013) *School self-evaluation for school improvement: What works and why?* CfBT. Available at: https://www.academia.edu/11341049/_School_self_evaluation_for_school_improvement_What_works_and_why_?email_work_card=thumbnail

23 Main, P. (nd) Ofsted: Past, Present And The Future. Blog post, *Structural Learning*. Available at: https://www.structural-learning.com/post/ofsted-past-present-and-the-future

24 NFER (2018) *What Impact Does Accountability Have On Curriculum, Standards and Engagement In Education? A Literature Review.* Available at: https://www.nfer.ac.uk/media/3032/nfer_accountability_literature_review_2018.pdf

in education, while on the other, accountability systems may produce negative effects, 'making it more difficult for schools to deliver the sought after quality', themes which will also be explored later in this book.

CHAPTER 3
THE ROLE OF OFSTED

By 'inspection' is meant the process of seeing a school at work in the course of its ordinary routine ... what is the course of education, physical and intellectual ... what is the order and discipline; what the relations of the scholars, to their teachers, and to one another; how the teachers give their lessons ...

Taken from *School Inspection* by D. R. Fearon, 1876[25]

WHAT IS OFSTED AND WHAT IS ITS PURPOSE?

Ofsted is the Office for Standards of Education, Children's Services and Skills. It is responsible for inspecting and regulating education and training for learners of all ages, and also responsible for inspecting and regulating services which care for children and young people.

OFSTED OVER TIME

1992 – Established as the Office for Standards in Education. All schools would be inspected in a four-yearly cycle. Schools had six to ten weeks' notice of inspections.

1998 – Ofsted could inspect Local Authorities (LAs).

---

25   Fearon, D. R. (1876) *School Inspection*. London: Macmillan.

2000 – Ofsted could inspect Further Education (FE) colleges and school sixth forms, as well as nursery education and childcare settings, and became responsible for the approved childminder register.

2005 – Schools had two days' notice of inspections. Schools had to keep their own self-evaluation reports for Ofsted teams to refer to.

2007 – New title as remit expanded to include children's services work – Office for Standards in Education, Children's Services and Skills – combining the Commission for Social Care Inspection (CSCI), the Adult Learning Inspectorate (ALI), and the Family Court Advisory and Support Service (CAFCASS).

Before 1992 schools were inspected by their Local Education Authorities (LEAs). Ofsted was created under the Education (Schools) Act 1992 to centralise the school inspection system in response to 'inconsistent standards across the country and concerns over the independence of inspectors of local chief education officers and councillors'.[26] This Act also saw the introduction of the National Curriculum and the publication of league tables.

There are similar bodies in Wales (Estyn), Northern Ireland (the Education and Training Inspectorate in Northern Ireland (ETI)), and in Scotland (His Majesty's Inspectorate of Education in Scotland (HMiE)).

There have been many changes to the accountability of schools in England since 1988, as shown below.[27]

1988 – Education Reform Act (1988) introduced:
- the national curriculum
- key stages of education
- local management of schools

---

26 Politics.co.uk (2023) *Ofsted*. Available at: https://www.politics.co.uk/reference/ofsted/

27 NAHT (2018) *Improving School Accountability. Report of the NAHT Accountability Commission.* Available at: https://www.naht.org.uk/Portals/0/PDF's/Improving%20school%20accountability.pdf?ver=2021-04-27-121950-093/

- city technology colleges – grant-maintained schools beyond local authority control
- GCSE qualifications.

1991 – First statutory assessments based on national curriculum levels introduced.

1992 – Office for Standards in Education created (Ofsted) by Education (Schools) Act.

1992 – Annual performance tables introduced.

1994 – Introduction of A* GCSE grade.

1997 – Key Stage 3 SATs introduced.

2000 – Learning and Skills Act provided for the establishment of the first city academies, later known as sponsored academies. AS-levels introduced.

2001 – Ofsted's inspection remit expanded to include day-care and childminding.

2002 – Value-added progress measure introduced.

2005 – Education Act designed to strengthen accountability framework for schools:

- More frequent, shorter inspections.
- Definitions for inadequate schools (special measures/significant improvement).
- Statutory intervention powers for local authorities. Ofsted introduced a self-evaluation form for schools.

2006 – Education and Inspections Act introduced new powers for school intervention and changes to the functions of Ofsted and the Chief Inspector. Value-added progress measure replaced with contextual value-added measure.

2008 – A* grade introduced at A-level.

2009 – Ofsted introduced a new inspection framework. Key Stage 3 SATs discontinued.

2010 – Academies Act provided powers for the Secretary of State to make an academy order to create a sponsored academy (including a free school, studio school or UTC) and for maintained schools to 'convert' to become academies. EBacc introduced. Contextual value-added measure replaced with expected progress.

2011 – Education Act provided for:

- the exemption of most 'outstanding' schools from inspection
- changes to the matters to be covered in the inspection report.

2012 – Ofsted introduced a new inspection framework in January. Ofsted replaced the January framework in September, introducing a 'requires improvement' judgement, monitoring inspections of 'requires improvement' schools and the three-strikes rule.

2014 – New national curriculum introduced and levels removed.

2015 – One-day short inspections of 'good' schools introduced. Revision of all GCSE subjects including replacement of A* – G, with 9 – 1 grading. Introduction of new linear A-levels and start of separation of A- and AS-levels. Final reporting of levels for SATs and teacher assessment tests.

2016 – Interim pre-key stage standards introduced in place of P scales. New national curriculum tests introduced. Progress 8 measure introduced. Scaled scores introduced to measure school level progress in primary schools.

2018 – Significant changes to short inspection arrangements to reduce the number converted to full inspections. The three-strikes rule for 'requires improvement' schools dropped. Pre-key stage standards formally replace P scales.

2019 – Final examinations for 'unreformed' A-level courses.

2020 – All GCSE, AS- and A-level awards will conform to new requirements.

This timeline clearly demonstrates that Ofsted regularly reviews its own work, and believes it consults on any changes it wishes to make. It has piloted inspection frameworks before they have been rolled out, and it would claim to be reflective and responsive to concerns. However, it is often the unintended consequences of its changes that have huge ramifications and increase pressure within the system. Senior staff rewriting the formats for school development plans, self-evaluation documents, and all the work that goes into impact statements to prove curriculums are ambitious, to name but a few.

Adrian Gray in his book *European School Inspection and Evaluation*[28] sets out the following as reasons why we inspect:

- National priorities change over time because society changes and education does not exist within a political vacuum.

- It is the role of inspectorates to reflect these changing priorities as part of a democratic system.

- Priorities may change, and some may be temporary, but other aspects of inspection are remarkably consistent.

The first point here raises an interesting question. If we agree that education exists in a political sphere, and that national priorities change because society changes, then does this mean we are inspecting and monitoring to ensure the will of the government (and by extension, the populace) is being enforced? Taken to its ultimate extension this is no doubt true, as the government sets the parameters for success and failure which Ofsted must adhere to. Gray's second point then follows that it is of course for Ofsted to check that schools have listened and taken on board these changing priorities – The literacy and numeracy strategies are a good example of this, and many have agreed that the 2015 framework focus on pupil premium children was a good idea. His third point lays out that while there will be some changes due to who is in power and what their educational ideology is, much of the frameworks stay the same – such as ensuring the safety of the pupils.

---

28   Gray, A. (2019) *European School Inspection and Evaluation*. Nottingham: Bookworm of Retford.

Writing about inspections in countries across Europe, Gray suggests that 'inspection can both evaluate schools and contribute to their improvement' although this doesn't seem applicable to the English model as we have very limited evidence of a link between inspection and improvement, as suggested by McGill.[29] And rather interestingly, Gray asks, 'can you both offer advice and hold schools to account?' Should Ofsted inspect schools to judge their effectiveness and at the same time publish research about what it holds up as good school improvement practice?

According to Paul Main, 'The role of Ofsted is to promote excellent care and education in England. Reporting directly to the government, Ofsted pride themselves on being impartial and independent.'[30] Do we all see the role of Ofsted as slightly different? An improvement agency? An inspectorate? A regulatory body? Do they even know who they are?

HOW DOES OFSTED WORK?

In its latest strategy document[31] Ofsted opens with 'Ofsted aims to improve lives by raising standards in education and children's social care'. It clearly sets out its belief that Ofsted is a 'force for improvement' whose key aims are, 'raising standards and improving lives.' We will come back to this claim throughout the book. The strategy lists four values, as shown below.

---

29   McGill, R. M. (2022) Ofsted is not effective in driving school improvement. Blog post. *Teacher Toolkit.* Available at: https://www.teachertoolkit.co.uk/2022/07/31/ofsted-school-improvement/

30   Main, P. (nd) Ofsted: Past, Present And The Future. Blog post, *Structural Learning.* Available at: https://www.structural-learning.com/post/ofsted-past-present-and-the-future

31   Ofsted (2022) *Ofsted strategy 2022-27.* Available at: https://www.gov.uk/government/publications/ofsted-strategy-2022-to-2027/ofsted-strategy-2022-27

1. CHILDREN AND LEARNERS FIRST

Our focus is on improving outcomes for children and learners. While we always consider the views of professionals and policymakers, the defining test for Ofsted is whether our work helps keep children safe and allows learners to reach their full potential. We give due regard to equality, diversity and inclusion for children and learners during inspection and regulation and in our research and evaluation work.

2. INDEPENDENT

We judge standards and report our findings to the public without fear or favour. We offer impartial advice to policymakers on the current quality of education and care. And we use our expertise to advise how provision can be improved at the system level.

3. ACCOUNTABLE AND TRANSPARENT

We report to Parliament on how we carry out our inspection and regulatory functions and how we spend taxpayers' money. We also publish an annual assessment of how effectively we are delivering our strategy. We are transparent: our approach to regulation and inspection is open to scrutiny.

4. EVIDENCE-LED

Our policies, frameworks, judgements and insights are rooted in evidence. We are proportionate and responsible in how we use our voice, providing the evidence to highlight significant issues.

It would be hard to argue with these values and what they represent, but how well are they being realised? Is Ofsted independent? Not everyone would agree, and many would say Ofsted is so closely aligned to political thinking – echoing Gray's views that 'education does not exist in a political vacuum' – that it would seem improbable they can be truly impartial. Accountable and transparent? Yes, they do write several reports and the Chief HMI has to report to Parliament for regular scrutiny, but there is growing discourse from headteachers that some inspector activity is not always that transparent, with many feeling inspectors come into schools with hidden agendas and preconceived ideas. Finally, evidence-led? Possibly the most misleading claim. They claim to be engaged in research and as the 2019 paper *The Education inspection framework – Overview of research* would suggest, they do draw on academic research (citing 236 sources). But do they cherry pick what matches their thinking? Before scientific articles are published, they are help up to strong scrutiny, do Ofsted do the same?

Then there are their strategic priorities:

- Inspections that raise standards
- Right-touch regulation
- Making the most of our insights
- The best start in life
- Keeping children safe
- Keeping pace with sector changes
- Accessible and engaged
- A skilled workforce

There is so much to comment on here. Do inspections raise standards? Chapter 5 examines this in detail and asks which standards are being referred to. Schools changing category or improved student outcomes? Or improvements in teaching and learning? Or recruitment and retention of staff? Many would ask and argue about what 'right-touch regulation' actually means, and who decides what is 'right' for whom. Safeguarding is an interesting one and one that is hard to reconcile with the fact that for so long 'outstanding' schools were exempt from inspection. As for the workforce, I doubt many would suggest inspectors were not highly skilled, though some would argue about issues round bias and subjectivity as well as inspectors going into schools with no experience of that phase of education, or even the setting, such as special schools.

By focusing on these strategic priorities, Ofsted hope to achieve 22 outcomes, including:

- Over 90% of providers will agree that their inspection will help them improve standards.

- More providers demonstrate good or outstanding leadership and management from the start, with fewer judged less than good at their first inspection and a reduction in repeated enforcement action.

- Practice will improve because stakeholders and inspectors use our insights, with an increase in the percentage of stakeholders who have read and used our research.

- Early years practice will improve because practitioners use our research, evidenced by feedback from focus groups with the sector.

There is definitely a continuing theme around engagement with research and leading research but, as I discuss later, I wonder if this is confusing the roles of Ofsted as a force for improvement and a regulatory body. The strategy also suggests that Ofsted will review the effectiveness of the framework; I am sure we are all waiting to see what the next framework will look like and where the emphasis will lie. If, as Gray suggests 'National priorities change over time because society changes and education does not exist within a political vacuum', then maybe this is where we should be looking for hints about the future.

CHANGING OFSTED

In the last few years Ofsted have been keen to show themselves as an evidence-led and evidence-informed organisation, and, over time, there have been a number of changes to inspection and Ofsted in England[32] These include:

- The introduction of short inspections for most good schools and non-exempt outstanding schools in September 2015, instead of full Section 5 inspections.

- The introduction of a new Common Inspection Framework for education, skills and early years in 2015.

- Between 2013 and 2018, the commissioning of batched or focused inspections of schools in the same multi-academy trust (MAT),

---

32   Roberts, N. and Hill, R. (2021) *School inspections in England: Ofsted.* London: House of Commons Library.

reflecting the changing landscape of school organisation in England.

- From 2018, the introduction of MAT summary evaluations with the first evaluation report published in February 2019.
- In recent years, an increased focus on identifying and tackling unregistered independent schools.
- The introduction of a new Education Inspection Framework from September 2019.
- In November 2020, the removal of the existing exemption from routine inspection for mainstream schools judged outstanding.
- The suspension of most routine school inspections during the coronavirus pandemic and their resumption from the autumn 2021 term.

Review and reform are welcome. There have been calls for 'review, reform or replace', and while Ofsted certainly wouldn't agree with the last one, this must surely be the time for them to review and reform once again. I believe many of us want an accountability approach that works, one that is fair, forward thinking, reasonable and understands context. Is this too much to ask?

THE CURRENT FRAMEWORK

The framework itself has also changed over time. The most recent version puts a greater emphasis on curriculum and has moved away from what some say was a focus on school data and outcomes. These changes arose from Ofsted's own consultation on the current framework in 2019.[33] Some of their findings, as summarised by Paul Main are outlined below.

---

33 Ofsted (2019) *Consultation outcome. Education inspection framework 2019: a report on the responses to the consultation.* Available at: https://www.gov.uk/government/ consultations/education-inspection-framework-2019-inspecting-the-substance- of-education/outcome/education-inspection-framework-2019-a-report-on-the- responses-to-the-consultation

- The accountability system has skewed the ways schools operate. School leaders have unintentionally given a higher weighting to Maths and English at the expense of other subjects. This detrimental approach has improved results in core subjects, but experts fear the real substance of education and child development has suffered.

- Spreadsheets of performance data have become overemphasised, and in some contexts, damaging to the mental health of both students and staff. The headlines are filled with stories of senior leaders feeling compelled to leave their posts because of this unintentional problem. For many Head Teachers, real outcomes cannot always be put into an Excel database.

- The average tenure for a teacher is three years. The biggest reason for staff shortage is workload, and, in many cases, unnecessary workload. Teaching staff work hard and work with purpose. The biggest frustration is being asked to do things purely for reasons relating to accountability when they could be doing something more impactful.

- Results are important, no one is denying this. What Ofsted noticed was a pattern of 'teaching for the test'. School teachers felt compelled to front-load shallow short-term knowledge at the expense of deeper expertise that would be useful beyond school. Time pressures were documented a lot and many teachers who were up against exam deadlines felt that they had no choice other than to just deliver facts. Students who were often at the negative receiving end of these practices were disadvantaged learners.[34]

Ofsted have demonstrated that it does seek stakeholder views and this consultation in 2019 gathered more than 15,000 responses relating to proposed changes to the framework and key judgement areas. Ofsted then changed the framework, which was widely welcomed, but as expected these changes led to another raft of different pressures that Ofsted had not

---

34 Main, P. (nd) Ofsted: Past, Present And The Future. Blog post, *Structural Learning*. Available at: https://www.structural-learning.com/post/ofsted-past-present-and-the-future

fully anticipated. As mentioned, the focus on intent, implementation and impact has seen many schools rewrite curriculum policies and website pages, and as for learning journey maps – I am sure many of us learned new skills with drawing roads and paths on different apps!

In a speech to the Schools North East Summit in October 2018, Ofsted's Chief Inspector, Amanda Spielman, discussed the reasoning behind the proposals for the 2019 education inspection framework:

> It is clear that, for some time, Ofsted hasn't placed enough emphasis on the curriculum. For a long time, our inspections have looked hardest at outcomes, placing too much weight on test and exam results when we consider the overall effectiveness of schools. The cumulative impact of performance tables and inspections and the consequences that are hung on them has increased the pressure on school leaders, teachers and indirectly on pupils to deliver perfect data above all else.
>
> But we know that focusing too narrowly on test and exam results can often leave little time or energy for hard thinking about the curriculum, and in fact can sometimes end up making a casualty of it.
>
> The bottom line is that we must make sure that we, as an inspectorate, complement rather than intensify performance data, because our curriculum research and a vast amount of sector feedback have told us that a focus on performance data is coming at the expense of what is taught in schools.
>
> A new focus on substance should change that, bringing the inspection conversation back to the substance of young people's learning and treating teachers like the experts in their field, not just data managers. I don't know a single teacher who went into teaching to get the perfect progress 8 score. They go into it because they love what they teach and want children to love it too. That is where the inspection conversation should start and with the new framework, we have an opportunity to do just that.
>
> This is why we will be proposing a new judgement of quality of education as one of 4 judgements in our new framework.

PROPOSED CHANGES

In fact at the top level, there are 3 main proposed changes. The first change is losing outcomes as a standalone judgement. The second change is broadening the existing quality of teaching, learning and assessment judgement into a quality of education judgement. This one should include curriculum alongside teaching, learning and assessment, and will also reflect outcomes. Then third, we propose splitting the current judgement of personal development, behaviour and welfare into 2 separate judgements: one for behaviour and attitudes and the other for personal development.

Under quality of education, we intend to look at 3 distinct aspects. First the intent – what is it that schools want for all their children? Then the implementation – how is teaching and assessment fulfilling the intent? Finally, the impact – that is the results and wider outcomes that children achieve and the destinations that they go on to.

We believe that this new judgement will allow Ofsted to recognise primary schools that, for example, prioritise phonics and the transition into early reading, and which encourage older pupils to read widely and deeply. And it will make it easier for secondary schools to do the right thing, offering children a broad range of subjects and encouraging the take-up of core EBacc subjects such as the humanities and languages at GCSE, alongside the arts and creative subjects.

At the same time, Ofsted will challenge those schools where too much time is spent on preparation for tests at the expense of teaching, where pupils' choices are narrowed or, as mentioned above, where children are pushed into less rigorous qualifications mainly to boost league table positions.

By separating 'personal development, welfare and behaviour' into 2 judgements, we are recognising the very different elements at stake here. We believe that the tough business of behaviour and the attitudes pupils bring to learning and a school's approach to things like attendance, bullying and exclusions are best considered separately from the question of pupils' wider personal development, such as the

> opportunities they have to learn about being active, healthy and engaged citizens. And as I said, leadership and management is also expected to remain a key area of consideration.[35]

Roberts and Hill looked at reactions to the consultation. They comment on the response from the NAHT which said that while it welcomed the 'shift in emphasis towards a more detailed examination of a school's curriculum and a reduced focus on data', the proposals did not 'fulfil the recommendations the union had made in its September 2018 Accountability Commission report'. Roberts and Hill also found that, 'The Education Policy Institute (EPI) think tank praised many aspects of the new framework, including its focus on off-rolling and schools' use of exclusion. However, it criticised Ofsted's decision to stop recommending that some schools review their use of the Pupil Premium, and for the framework's approach to speaking and listening skills in the early years and in the teaching of early reading.' Roberts and Hill refer to a piece in *The Guardian* by commentator Warwick Mansell who 'outlines the arguments around whether the framework's emphasis on developing cultural capital could be viewed as dismissing the experiences of working-class children'. They found that, 'Multi Academy Trust CEOs have also criticised perceived Ofsted resistance to 3 year GCSEs, arguing that judging against schools pursuing a lengthier key stage 4 phase will "damage outcomes for disadvantaged children".'[36]

Spielman also addressed disadvantage in her 2018 speech:

'I believe that one of the limitations of the current accountability system is the incentive, perhaps even pressure, for schools to put overall results ahead of individual children's needs. ... Few schools don't feel that pervasive undercurrent and for schools serving disadvantaged children, the pull can be stronger. ... We also know that these undesirable incentives sometimes lie behind pupils coming off school rolls. And, sadly, it is disproportionately the more disadvantaged children who are affected.

---

35 Spielman, A. (2019) *Speech to Schools North East Summit.* Delivered 11 October 2018. Available at: https://www.gov.uk/government/speeches/amanda-spielman-speech-to-the-schools-northeast-summit

36 Roberts, N. and Hill, R. (2021) *School inspections in England: Ofsted.* London: House of Commons Library.

… We are already increasing the focus on off-rolling under our existing framework.'[37] School leaders have welcomed the acceptance that some schools have been 'gaming the system' and are glad that attention has been brought to this.

The consultation summary and proposal had put curriculum at the focus of the latest framework, and this was welcomed by many.

Daisy Christodoulou suggests the current (2022) framework makes a big difference to the work schools do on curriculum. In an interview for the Chartered College of Teaching (CCT) she says that the current framework's focus on curriculum allows us to have a deeper, more intellectual and philosophical focus on the curriculum, what schools are hoping to achieve and how they are hoping to achieve this. She believes it helps teachers think about and share their love for their own subjects with students and how they work to improve students' understanding of their subjects. She highlights that this framework allows the curriculum to drive assessment, not the other way around. There are comments about the possibility of unintended consequences, which although not explored in this short interview, seems to be a common concern.[38] Many school leaders have reported on inspectors fixated by what children can remember – can they 'know and do more'? But asking a six-year-old – or even a teenager – what they learned yesterday or last week may not be the best way to ensure children have learned things and stored them in their long-term memory!

However, writing for *Schools Week*, David Scott questions the effect of the changes and highlights that many leaders call for different frameworks for different educational phases. He writes: 'the framework is at the epicentre of the problem. It is clearly unfit for purpose in the lower primary age range and early years, its "outstanding" criteria mainly unattainable due to a secondary model-dominated, subject-driven, knowledge-based agenda.' He adds that, 'subject leaders in first and infant schools are being interrogated with the

---

37 Spielman, A. (2019) *Speech to Schools North East Summit*. Delivered 11 October 2018. Available at: https://www.gov.uk/government/speeches/amanda-spielman-speech-to-the-schools-northeast-summit

38 CCT (nd) *Find out what Daisy Christodoulou thinks about the new Ofsted framework*. Interview by the CCT with Daisy Christodoulou (video). Available at: https://my.chartered.college/research-hub/find-out-what-daisy-christodoulou-thinks-about-the-new-ofsted-framework/ (login required).

same questions as secondary heads of department. The crucial difference is that the former are responsible for delivering the whole curriculum with limited non-contact time to develop and monitor a subject throughout the school. They succeed in most subjects, but inspectors can usually find at least one that is not perfect to justify a downgrade.' He goes on to say, 'a further anomaly is that Ofsted's inspection of providers on the early years register uses a different framework, that is specific and more suited to that age range. This enables many of these settings to attain higher grades than local authority school-based reception and nursery classes. This is unfair to the schools, and confusing for parents and carers.'[39]

This is a growing criticism: should frameworks be written for the different phases? We have additional guidance and criteria for EYFS and sixth form, but the phases are remarkably different and unique. Can one single framework really articulate what is best practice for all ages from three to 16 years?

Let us consider then if it is the framework or the process that causes stresses in the systems. In the opening chapter of this book we heard that some people say inspectors are inconsistent and judgements are inconsistent, but many people say the current framework is the best yet as it has moved away from a focus on outcomes to a focus on provision – what schools hope to achieve for their young people and how they will support their well-being. The focus on curriculum rather than outcomes is better. The focus on SMSC and wellbeing, looking at opportunities to develop the 'whole child' is more centre stage and few disagree that this is an improvement. There have however been issues with how some providers have interpreted the framework, and some schools' obsession with intent and implementation has caused huge workload increases for senior and middle leaders. There are few school websites which don't use these words intent and implementation now, and a whole industry of preparing middle leaders for deep dives has sprung up. In fact, Ofsted's updated framework in September 2022 acknowledges this and changed the language and layout of the framework in response to this obsession on the part of some individuals and institutions.

---

39   Scott, D. (2022) Ofsted's framework is failing first and infant schools. *Schools Week*. 16 October. Available at: https://schoolsweek.co.uk/ofsteds-framework-is-failing-first-and-infant-schools/

CHAPTER 4
PRESSURES IN THE SYSTEM

CAN YOU EVER BE READY FOR AN INSPECTION?

Some might say yes, but I've always wanted just a few more days, or a few more weeks. When I have met with the inspectors during Ofsted visits I have spoken with them about what's been written into our school development plan (SDP) and they have acknowledged this in terms of leadership capacity. But this can only go as far as proving we know what we need to do; it doesn't prove we have actually started to do it or seen initial impacts from our efforts. Inspectors like to see things happening, in action, even if they are only just beginning to be implemented. There's little more frustrating than being asked why you don't have something in place already when your rollout plan for that 'something' is scheduled to start next Monday. There are other views about the timing of visits, with some schools seemingly well prepared and eager for the inspection to happen. This type of school feels 'ready' and their only frustration comes when they keep having to wait.

Preparation for Ofsted is overwhelming. A lot of the work that prepares a school for the inspection goes on under the surface. Many hours, weeks and months of work go into preparing staff at all levels, but especially middle leaders and, increasingly, pastoral teams (with the current framework) for the sorts of questions they may be asked during inspection interviews. Mocksteds, practise deep dives, work scrutiny, learning walks and stakeholder voice, all in full flow and rehearsal mode. This all happens partly to prepare people and partly to identify any weakness or areas of concern to school leaders rather than Ofsted, and also partly for reassurance for the leadership team. Safeguarding, and checks on safeguarding, are constantly reviewed, quite rightly. Some senior teams even have leaders whose sole responsibility is to be inspection ready. What a role! The money being spent on employing consultants and teams from other schools to come in and 'help' with all this Ofsted preparation is extraordinary, but the stakes are so high that many leaders feel it is very much worth it. I have known one school which paid seven consultants to come in weekly for two terms; couldn't this money be better directed towards the school itself? And what a pressure on staff; receiving advice from, and being accountable to, so many people at one time. This is something else that explains the current exodus of teachers from the profession: too much top-down accountability and too little autonomy and trust given to these professionals – the staff already working in these schools.

I've recently looked at a document one 'supporting' school made for another, the former having just been through an Ofsted, the latter awaiting theirs. The first school, as if it hadn't been enough work for them having just had the inspection, created more work for themselves by putting some training together to share their experience with the second. I think this is great practice insofar as this school is willing to help another, and I am a huge fan of schools helping schools, but when we ask if inspection creates additional workload, even this type of activity brings unintended consequences and creates more work for someone.

The training offered was welcomed, of course, and included a range of information which the second school should consider:

- How senior leaders should prepare before an inspection looking at curriculum reviews.

- Training for middle leaders on how to be prepared to speak to inspectors about their own curriculums.

- Examples of curriculum documents from different departments.

- Models of different types of 'deep dives' with practice questions.

- Preparation questions for department staff, not just the head of department.

- Information to leaders on how to plan and manage the inspection visit itself.

- Practice questions for the initial call between the headteacher and the lead inspector.
- How senior leaders should behave through the inspection itself.

This list is not exhaustive, but it is definitely exhausting.

One blog I came across gave a list of questions that might be asked in the initial 90-minute phone call between the lead inspector and the headteacher:[40]

Curriculum	• What was involved in creating the vision for the school?
	• Give me a timeline of how your curriculum came about?
	• How does the motto of the school fit in with the intent and the implementation of the curriculum?
	• How does your commitment to the disadvantaged fit into the curriculum?
	• How is your curriculum sequenced?
	• What does this look like in real terms – how is this implemented?
	• What is the subject knowledge of the teachers like?
	• How do the subject leaders ensure that they sustain the knowledge and expertise of the teachers?
	• How has professional development fed into the implementation of the curriculum?
	• How do you know your curriculum is having an impact?
	• How do the leaders support the teachers?
	• How do you ensure that the students apply previous learning to current and future learning?
	• How do you ensure the children learn the key facts and acquire subject knowledge?
	• How does the teacher ensure the quality of long-term sequential planning and how is this implemented in real terms?
	• How are you checking that students know what they have learned?
	• How does the curriculum intent reflect the context and the most common barriers to learning?
	• How do you promote the love of reading – what will I see when I go to the classrooms? (Charlie's Challenge)
	• How do you promote the wellbeing of the staff?
	• How do you manage the workload of the staff?

40 Garvey, P. (2020) Questions asked in the 90-minute phone call to schools in #EIF2019. Blog post. *QA South-West*. 22 January. Available at: https://www.quality-schools.com/questions-asked-in-the-90-minute-phone-call-to-schools-in-eif2019/

	• How do you ensure that all children have access to the same educational input? • How are opportunities and equality accessed by all groups? • How is diversity celebrated and how does it run through the curriculum?
Personal development	• In what depth is this coherently planned and sequenced? • How aligned is the approach and delivery to the overall curriculum intent? • How consistent and embedded is the provision? What is the impact on pupils? • How are links made within and between subjects to enhance pupils' SMSC development? • Do pupils benefit from first-hand, memorable experiences as a basis for learning in context? • How are pupils' talents and interests identified and developed? • How does the provision reflect the school/community context?
Behaviour and attitudes	• How are strategies clearly communicated and consistently implemented? • How effective is training for all teaching and support staff? • Can students articulate how positive behaviour and attitudes are developed/encouraged/rewarded? • How are you encouraging attendance and punctuality? What is the impact? • Can we demonstrate that FTEs are a 'last resort'? • How do we develop pupils' resilience, independence, communication and risk awareness/risk-taking? Including when tasks are demanding, particularly for most able pupils. • Is attendance improving and where are any areas where attendance is high for particular groups?
Leadership and management	• Are leaders' ambitions/expectations of what all pupils (including SEND, DA, vulnerable groups) can achieve consistently high? • Is there a tangible, consistent culture of safeguarding? How do you know? • Are all staff aware of local and/or academy-specific vulnerabilities/safeguarding issues? • How do leaders check that all staff understand the previous question and act swiftly in response to all concerns/signs of vulnerability and risk as a result? • How do leaders ensure that newly appointed staff have the knowledge and understanding to keep children safe, particularly if training was completed elsewhere? • How are NQTs and newly appointed staff supported? Particularly in relation to academy-specific pedagogy, approaches, and policies. • How do leaders decide on policy/procedure content? E.g. curriculum, marking, planning.

	• What measures are taken to ensure staff are well supported? How do we ensure that meaningful engagement takes place with staff at all levels, including re: workload? • Do those responsible for governance understand their statutory duties? • Are those responsible for governance able to link questions/challenges and visits to key improvement priorities? • Do those responsible for governance hold leaders to account by following up responses to questions/challenges? Including by looking at evidence first-hand.

Don't you feel exhausted and nervous just reading this? I completely understand the need to feel ready and informed about what might be asked, but it's terrifying to think all this needs to be known and remembered! The work that has gone into this sort of preparation is extensive and often most welcomed by the receiving schools. I have even produced and gone through similar support myself. Some schools have really benefited in being more 'Ofsted ready' and it has been immensely helpful for them. However, what about the schools who do not get this support, advice and practice? This, along with the fact that some serving headteachers are inspectors, creates an uneven playing field, particularly in light of the controversy surrounding the inspector crib sheets. Although the crib sheets have now been made public, it is easy to understand how a system where there were some schools in which the headteacher had access to a list of exactly what Ofsted was looking for, while others did not, might be seen as inequitable.

Of course, all schools want to do well in inspections, and many put themselves through all this additional pressure and workload to be able to perform well on the day. My 'Iceberg' model shown in figure 6 tries to represent some of the additional work schools do just for the inspection as well as the normal work of the school trying to improve standards, and the existing external pressures it faces.

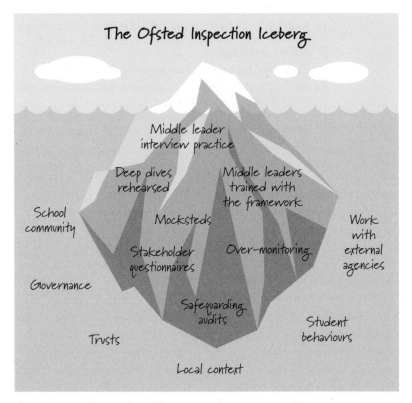

Figure 6. The Ofsted inspection iceberg

All of the work done inside the iceberg – preparing for Ofsted – prevents the school spending time on its own improvement agenda. When the Ofsted visits starts, if the visit is going well then above water is the calm environment of an effective school. If it's not going so well, then the waters can become a bit choppier. If less of this extra workload and Ofsted preparation work has been done, the iceberg might become less stable, and inspectors will see this. What if all the work inside the iceberg relating to inspection visits could disappear, and be replaced solely with the work the school knows will focus on its learners and its staff, rather than inspection preparation? The school could focus on what was going on in the sea, with the purpose of keeping it calm and easy to navigate. And then every now and then a small boat, maybe a peer review school, could come along and say, 'hey how's things, need any help?'

WHAT ABOUT DURING THE INSPECTION ITSELF?

Schools now 'get the call' the day before an inspection team arrives at the gates. This initial call is pretty formulaic and includes a range of questions, including the size of the school, details about the student population, the governance arrangements and if the school has a specialist resource provision. Even for experienced leaders this in itself can feel like the first part of the 'exam'. I know it has certainly felt like that to me.

There are two types of inspection: a Section 5 and a Section 8. A Section 5 is a graded inspection, known as a full inspection. A Section 8 inspection is ungraded and is generally a monitoring visit following a previous inspection, either where concerns have been raised or there is improvement work to be done, or to ensure the school remains 'good' or 'outstanding'.

During the visit the Ofsted team engage in a range of activities. Inspectors will spend time observing lessons and gathering evidence to inform their judgements. They will talk to a range of pupils and staff, including governors, about important aspects of the school's work. They have also been known to talk to parents at the school gates. Inspectors try to get a full view of the school over this brief visit and spend time out of the classroom at break times and lesson changeovers. It might be that initial conversations with school leaders or data investigations drive some lines of inquiry, but these may change over the course of a visit. Deep dives have become a real fashion where an inspector looks carefully at a particular subject or area, quite a scary proposition for staff new to middle leadership. Ofsted also collect questionnaires from staff, parents and, where possible, students. All the data they collect over the visit helps inform their thoughts and decisions about the separate – and then overall – judgements they award the school. There are various 'keeping in touch' visits between the lead inspector and the headteacher over the inspection to discuss how things are going. I find these meetings very useful in enabling me to see which way the inspectors are leaning and whether I feel they need to see additional practice in any area to help support their understanding of the school. At the end of the visit is the final debriefing where the lead inspector tells the leaders and members of the governing body or Trust what the judgement is. Pure pin drop moments, and sometimes a few tears of either relief, joy, sadness or utter heartbreak. The judgement is given but leaders are told to keep it secret as it needs to go back through Ofsted's own quality assurance processes before it is written up in a draft report, which is usually sent to the school within 18 days. This period is incredibly tricky depending on the outcome – everyone wants to know but leaders simply can't say.

This first draft report itself is only a few pages but summarises the strengths and areas of development for each area of the inspection framework. It awards a grade for each area and an overall grade is then awarded with a short section on what the school should do to improve. The school checks for accuracy, sends it back, then in a few more weeks the final report arrives. And that's it. The grade has been given and this will sit over the school for the next few years or in some cases, much longer.

I remember thinking, 'my name goes on this report!' and the high stakes nature of the process is magnified by this fact. There is simply no escaping it.

Schools behave in a variety of ways during the inspection itself: some make changes to what would have been happening in their school and some keep the school events as planned. I have heard of trips being cancelled, students told to stay home, leadership teams from other schools being called in to sit in remote offices offering advice throughout the day, and I am sure readers will all have their own examples of unusual activity! In my most recent inspection we had builders in during the morning fitting windows (pre-planned) and I remember panicking about safeguarding and health and safety all morning. In previous inspections I have been caught up with issues at the school gates talking with families, and even police officers, asking if they wouldn't mind moving their van away from outside the office where the inspectors were meeting. I have seen leaders cry when they receive the call and some to have gone home early after the call with the stress of it all.

Stress is a common response to the reality of an Ofsted visit, or even the mere thought of one. In figure 7 I have tried to map out how I think the levels of stress change over time. How leaders and schools react and respond to an Ofsted visit is entirely personal and individual, but over the years, and using my experience, I have generalised some of the ways our stress levels change and represented them on these graphs. When looked at alongside figure 6 it is no surprise that people feel the inspection regime needs to change.

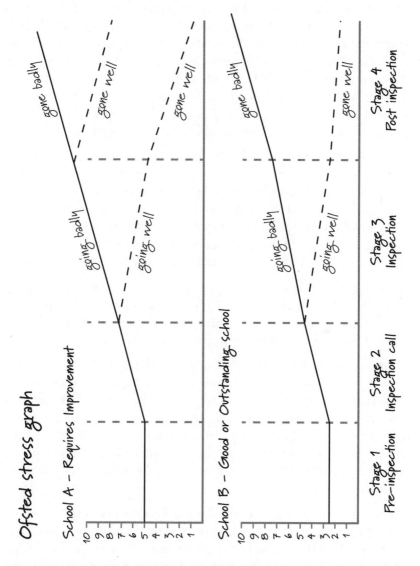

Figure 7. Changing stresses before, during and after an Ofsted inspection

The two graphs shown in figure 7 show differing tensions for the schools with different Ofsted judgements at the outset. School A, in the 'requires improvement' situation will have been working hard to improve, and achieving a better judgement will be of paramount importance to the school and its community, so stress levels are already higher. School B, which already has a 'good' or 'outstanding' judgement, although still concerned that it is seen to be continually improving, might be at a stage of slightly reduced stress before an inspection if it feels it is doing well. (It could in fact be at the same level of stress as the 'requires improvement' school if it feels it is at risk of being downgraded.) I appreciate this is not always the case, but I am trying to make a simple comparison.

At stage 1, school A is at a state of heightened tension. A better judgement is essential; to show the community it has improved and that parents should feel secure in deciding to send their children there, to demonstrate to the community that the local school is a good school, to show staff that all their efforts have been acknowledged as working and to give the pupils a new sense of pride in their own school. Added to all these pressures are those from above, from governors and Trust leaders.

School B might feel more secure in its existing judgement or it might be looking to achieve a better grade or better reading in the final report. If school B is really worried (maybe outcomes have fallen, staff have changed, or both) they may experience more of school A's journey.

Stage 2 indicates when the inspection call comes in. For both schools tension rises. Some leaders may feel more confident than others that the school is 'inspection ready' but due to the high-stakes nature of this event, most leaders are concerned about the inspection going well and the school achieving a good result. For small schools, this tension can often be more acute for the leader who has fewer people in their leadership team to turn to and delegate some of the inspection activities to.

In some schools, stage 2 brings real panic. Leaders may feel they are not quite ready if they haven't begun to implement plans or if it's too early to show impact from some of their improvement strategies, but there might also be panic about the inspection itself. Where will the inspectors go? Who will they talk to? What if that parent says this or this member of staff says that? What if Year 9 have a really bad day? What if the security gate isn't fixed by the morning?

In other schools the stress level might be lower, either because leaders and staff feel 'ok, we are ready', or 'well, there is nothing else we can do now'. The behaviour of the leader is very influential here on the stresses of the whole school. This is a time for real courage and calmness, or at least to show these attributes outwardly.

Stage 3 has equal strains. During the visit the inspectors see things and raise them at the keeping-in-touch meetings. Again, the behaviour of leaders is critical here in determining what happens next. If they calmly go on and find evidence for inspectors that proves or disproves their thinking, then this helps. If they leave the inspectors' room flapping and panicking then this feeling moves around the school building, making everyone feel on edge, and inspectors will pick up on this. Stage 3 is an interesting one, because as the inspection progresses it does become very clear what inspectors are looking for and what they are looking at. Leaders realise where judgements are going and can try to steer them towards the school's own desired endpoints. In some cases it becomes very obvious that the inspectors have come to judgements that cannot be shifted and that a school might either not move from 'requires improvement' or might be downgraded from an original 'good' or 'outstanding' grade.

It is important to consider the leader here. No amount of rhetoric around 'we are all in it together', 'it's the whole leadership team', or 'the governors are responsible for the strategic vision of the school' takes the pressure off the headteacher. As mentioned, it is their name that goes on the report. It can make or break careers. It stays with you as you move schools, and sadly it becomes a label that only a few take the time to unpick in conversations about future employment.

Then there is stage 4, the outcome. It's gone well, the stress is relieved. It hasn't gone well and the stress changes and turns into continuing pressure to do better next time. Bad judgements have caused people to quit or be asked to leave, and sadly much, much worse. Positive judgements cause celebration and a brief lull in stress before the next cycle begins. Anecdotally, bad judgements have also been used to make the whole staff workforce feel demoralised and I have heard tales of this type of response by school leaders to their staff following the announcement of final judgements:

We've all failed, and I hold you all personally responsible for this.

We've failed and that's down to everyone in this room. There will be some serious changes now. I'm utterly disappointed.

It is not surprising that this experience and this level of responsibility is putting many senior leaders off applying for headteacher roles, especially at a time when we need strong leaders the most (although arguably this is at all times). And of course there is the outcome that schools dread the most, that of being told you are 'inadequate'. Blunt and damning. The stress and sadness associated with this grade is simply awful. Far too many leaders I speak with would agree that the level of accountability that schools face actually leads to unnecessary workload, and this book is in direct response to this issue, following on from my last book, *School self-review – a sensible approach*.

Even students experience the associated pressures of Ofsted inspections. A group of school students worked with researchers from UCL and the organisation States of Mind – which advocates for new ways of thinking about mental health – on the project *Breaking the Silence*,[41] designed to capture the perspectives of students on how they thought their schools were assessed.[42] The project is ongoing, but has so far produced both the documentary film *The Framework*,[43] and a draft education evaluation framework, *The Review for Progress and Development*, designed to, 'provide an alternative to Ofsted's method of assessment that would provide an improved and more holistic way of judging schools.'[44]

---

41 States of Mind (2020) *What would an education inspection look like if students did the inspecting? We're finding out*. Available at: https://www.statesofmind.org/journal/2020/11/18/education-inspection-students.html

42 States of Mind (nd) *Breaking the Silence*. Available at: https://www.statesofmind.org/breaking-the-silence

43 Ibid.

44 States of Mind (nd) *Draft – Review for Progress and Development*. Available at: https://docs.google.com/document/d/1hEL-zxtfMxke_AqBYXuRmGMZMHiE-0WQ/edit

The project was reported on by Fiona Millar of *The Guardian*, who wrote that some of the feelings and comments from the young people involved were directly about Ofsted, and that students recognised that, 'the more we investigated, the more we realised that the pressure of league tables and Ofsted creates anxiety and stress for pupils and teachers and makes the whole environment tense. No one likes being judged. We also found that pupils and teachers felt they behaved differently when Ofsted was in the school, so their findings may not even be accurate.' Having set up surveys and focus groups, students found that, 'a recurring response was that young people felt the inspection framework did not include enough opportunities for them to talk about their wellbeing and mental health.' The alternative Ofsted proposal included, 'an end to two-day inspections, which the researchers say do not give time to adequately capture the student voice, and no more grading of schools, which former Ofsted inspectors told them led to "game-playing".'

The students called for 'a model in which schools work in clusters, evaluate each other and rely more heavily on surveys and focus groups about mental health and wellbeing, pupil-teacher relationships and life skills'. When talking about inspections in schools and how students are superficially involved in surveys and student voice, one member of the project said, 'none of us felt we had the opportunity to contribute to inspections and the consensus was that Ofsted doesn't listen to students, and that does show.' When asked what they might say to Amanda Spielman, one young person said, 'I would say to her that the inspection framework has an impact on us all the time, not just when we have an inspection, because of the pressure it puts on teachers. It would be better if Ofsted looked at ways to improve rather than critique schools.'[45]

REAL EXPERIENCES

Everyone who works in or with a school, or, as above, is a student at a school will have a view about Ofsted. There are of course people who have 'dodged the bullet' of inspections throughout their career but they will all

45 Millar, F. (2022) Inspecting the inspectors: students assess Ofsted regime's toll on wellbeing. *The Guardian*. 29 July. Available at: https://www.theguardian.com/education/2022/jun/29/inspecting-the-inspectors-students-assess-ofsted-regimes-toll-on-wellbeing

know people who have not. I interviewed several people from different contexts when writing this book, their experiences vary but there are some common underlying themes in their views and feelings about inspection:

I'd been in the school for seven days as the new headteacher. I was in an unfamiliar place with unfamiliar staff and children. I didn't know the parents or the governors. I hadn't read all the policies. I didn't know the curriculum. I had checked safeguarding arrangements on my first day, but everything else was still treacle for me. I was just sitting down to make sense of the School Development Plan and I heard this voice, 'It's Ofsted on the phone.' You think you know how you'll react but I couldn't feel anything, not to start with, but over the next hour while I waited for the official pre-inspection call, the fear set in. Not so much the fear of the inspection, but the absolute fear of not knowing everything about my school, and the fear of looking at all the faces in the building and feeling I could let them all down.

New headteacher

I feel that the Ofsted framework has changed a lot over time. It used to be much more about teaching, with inspectors at the classroom doors grading lessons and talking about teaching approaches. I feel it's much more about the children now. With my role as Designated Safeguarding Lead I feel it's much more about safeguarding and looking at records. It's more about looking at how children develop rather than how they are taught. Schools now seem to be the whole community, with staff acting as teachers, social workers, counsellors, nurses, locum parents, mentors – child rearers in essence. Even parents pull on this and email in and ask the school to talk to their children for them. The Ofsted framework makes you feel like you are being measured on all this and all the stuff you can't control, like what's happening in the child's life outside school, but you are made to feel you should.

Deputy head in a large independent secondary and designated safeguarding lead

The pressure to be graded 'excellent' is overwhelming. Even if one of the categories is good, the sky falls in. The stress passes down to middle

leaders from 'above' and the core subject leaders especially feel this pressure and anxiety. We all have to write our own department self-evaluation documents so we are responsible fully for our areas. They have to be two pages and we all send them to the senior team. When the inspection is announced we need to write and send detailed lesson plans to the leadership team to check over before the inspectors come in. It's a lot of work. Our leadership self-evaluation document is over 25 pages long, and one of our leadership team has 'inspection' as part of their job description. It's big business in my school.

Middle leader in an independent school

Sometimes I wish the lessons were graded – then at least I'd know if I did my bit.

Classroom teacher

I feel like I just jump through hoops without doing anything meaningful. I feel it's me personally that is being tested, not the school provision itself. It's all very high stakes, and yet when you 'meet the standards', you don't even get a well done. The inspectors tick off the standards and walk off to their next meeting.

Deputy head

The stress of inspection doesn't end when the inspection ends. There's the politics. It seems an unfair thing that some of the school community such as governors and senior staff get to hear the outcome, but most don't. An incredibly hard-working middle leader who has thrown their all at the school and the process, who is desperate to have their efforts, their tears and their value validated, and you can't tell them the outcome officially. We know that there is a quality assurance process once the inspectors hand in their notes, but surely the time for getting the whole school together to share these judgments – subject to this QA process – should be immediate. Some leaders hint at the words, but only a few are confident that they've heard it. Some school leaders tell everyone but say not to tell, some say something and play caution. This is a bit divisive all round and should be changed. All staff should get to hear the outcome immediately but with an understanding this might change. I imagine it's because a few school judgments got changed and everyone was unhappy about it, but I cannot imagine that's common.

Headteacher

It seems the pastoral teams are much more involved than they were. The social, moral, spiritual and cultural (SMSC) inspection element is huge right now. There is a lot on the shoulders of the personal, social, health and emotional (PSHE) lead, along with the wider team of pastoral staff. I don't think this is wrong, but surely the main point of Ofsted should be to judge the education they get in the classroom?

Pastoral support worker

I don't see the need to have safeguarding inspected by both the local authority and inspection teams.

Designated safeguarding lead

Everyone knows it depends who you get. There is so much inconsistency with the inspectors themselves. The entire inspection is predicated on what the lead inspector is like. Some come with real preconceptions about a school context that they just don't seem to be able to see through or shrug off. I met one inspector who didn't understand the pace of my inner-city London school, the liveliness and the attitudes of some of our students who were not being rude, but were confident urban kids. I think it can be really difficult to understand how context matters. I've seen students challenge teachers in a really articulate, inquiring way, only to see they've been noted down as 'challenging' but not in the way I see it.

Deputy head, London secondary school

After the call I really did feel the burden lay solely with me. It felt like a burden, I can't describe that feeling in any other way. Being the headteacher of a small school means you really do need to know everything – but how could you know? Why would you not? I felt for my staff, again as a small school, each person had a big responsibility that sat with them. The maths lead was also the English lead as well as the SENCo. Not ideal. I knew the inspection framework inside out – or so I thought – I realised I was reading and interpreting it differently over those few days. The way the inspectors interpreted the different points was also slightly different to mine and I felt the sands shifting under my feet. I felt I had to 'prove' what was happening, not just talk about it, or show it. I felt a bit undermined as a professional, that my word wasn't good enough. My staff were challenged in a way I thought was too harsh and too impersonal. Some of my staff were understandably tearful. I felt guilty that I couldn't make conversations easier and less interrogatory. I knew I had to look like the strong one but I too was panicking inside. At one point I could see it all falling down. How could I let this happen? How could I be responsible for the failure of our school for our families and our children, and our community. I'm not scarred by the experience and it was okay in the end, but it wasn't enjoyable. I'm sure we can be held to account in a more humane way.

Headteacher of a small school

Last year I allowed my anxiety to get the better of me. I sat hour after hour at the kitchen table, after my family had gone to bed, trying to second guess what was in the mind of the Ofsted inspector I'd never met or even knew the name of. We were awaiting the call and I was at the very end of my 'Ofsted Cycle of Courageousness' (some of you may recognise this from a presentation you've heard me give).

I made myself ill because I wanted to make sure that the staff that work so very hard were rewarded and not punished for choosing to work in our context. They deserve recognition and not to be made to feel inadequate and I didn't want to be the thing that let them down.

Vic Goddard

While I fully recognise the need for, and understand the role of regulation in our schools this chapter has only scratched at the surface of the pressures in the system that Ofsted, as it currently operates, causes. Schools want to work to improve the outcomes and opportunities for young people, but this level of pressure is a hindrance, not a help, and it is certainly not an improvement lever.

CHAPTER 5
IS OFSTED WORKING?

Ofsted's mantra is 'raising standards, improving lives'. So, how is it doing? Is all the additional workload and stress worth it? If there was an evidence base to show direct causality between inspection and improved standards for all young people, then maybe it would be.

DOES OFSTED IMPROVE SCHOOLS?

The NFER, in its literature review *What impact does accountability have on curriculum, standards and engagement in education?* finds – like many commentators on the subject – a lack of evidence on which to base a judgement. 'There is a paucity of data and robust, quantitative evidence about the impact of accountability on the curriculum, standards, and teacher and pupil engagement. In particular, there is little robust evidence about accountability on teacher workload, and teacher and pupil well-being.'[46]

Mary Bousted suggests that maybe 'Ofsted regards every one of its frequently changing inspection frameworks as valid, and perhaps that is why it has done no research into what would appear to be a fundamental area of enquiry'. She adds that as such there is no evidence that inspection practices improve 'teaching quality and pupil learning'. She argues that the Ofsted strapline of 'raising standards, improving lives' can only be described as an aspiration.[47]

---

46 Brill, F., Grayson, H., Kuhn, L. and O'Donnell, S. (2018) *What Impact Does Accountability Have On Curriculum, Standards and Engagement In Education? A Literature Review.* Slough, NFER. Available at: https://www.nfer.ac.uk/media/3032/nfer_accountability_literature_review_2018.pdf
47 Bousted, M. (2022) *Support Not Surveillance.* Woodbridge: John Catt.

The NFER report outlines its understanding of accountability and its purpose: 'Conceptualisations of accountability tend to reflect the idea that the mechanism itself can be a dynamic agent of positive change' and 'the whole purpose of accountability is widely accepted as one of strengthening the education system, rather than confirming the status quo'.[48]

The key findings of the literature review are set out below.

ACCOUNTABILITY AND THE CURRICULUM

Where pupil performance is used as a high stakes accountability measure, there is concern that certain parts of the curriculum become privileged above others at school delivery level, due to so-called 'teaching to the test'. Some pupils may receive an impoverished experience of the school curriculum as a result of targeted teaching where accountability systems focus on 'borderline' or 'cliff edge' measures. Jurisdictions may make deliberate system-level reforms to curriculum structure and documentation, typically in response to benchmarking the outcomes of international system comparisons.

ACCOUNTABILITY AND STANDARDS

How accountability measures are carried out is important – the literature suggests three principles for a positive relationship between accountability and school effectiveness: – clarity over responsibilities – alignment of objectives at all levels of the system – transparency of criteria used for assessing performance. The application of accountability measures may increase the achievement gap (e.g. by focussing attention on the performance of 'borderline' pupils); or conversely they may be used to reduce the gap (e.g. by informing funding programmes for disadvantaged pupils).

ACCOUNTABILITY AND TEACHER AND PUPIL ENGAGEMENT

Teacher education can support teachers' engagement with assessment data to inform classroom teaching and learning. Pupils may become

---

48   Brill, F., Grayson, H., Kuhn, L. and O'Donnell, S. (2018) *What Impact Does Accountability Have On Curriculum, Standards and Engagement In Education? A Literature Review*. Slough, NFER. Available at: https://www.nfer.ac.uk/media/3032/nfer_accountability_literature_review_2018.pdf

> less engaged learners when undue emphasis is placed upon performance of some groups at the expense of others.[49]

Amanda Spielman did try to address some of these findings, and the 2019 framework intended to take these into account.

Ofsted's own main findings, *State-funded schools inspections and outcomes as at 31 August 2022* reveal:

- 88% of all schools are good or outstanding.
- Only 17% of previously exempt schools that had a graded inspection this year remained outstanding.
- 70% of schools previously judged to require improvement improved to good or outstanding.

	% Outstanding	% Good	% Requires improvement	% Inadequate
As at 31 Aug 2022 (21,725)	18	70	9	3
As at 31 Aug 2021 (21,724)	19	67	10	3
As at 31 Aug 2020 (21,776)	19	67	10	4
As at 31 Aug 2019 (21,807)	20	66	10	4
As at 31 Aug 2018 (21,762)	21	65	11	4
As at 31 Aug 2017 (21,707)	21	66	10	4
As at 31 Aug 2016 (21,664)	20	66	11	3
As at 31 Aug 2015 (21,758)	20	62	15	3
As at 31 Aug 2014 (21,750)	19	60	17	4
As at 31 Aug 2013 (21,732)	19	57	20	3
As at 31 Aug 2012 (21,970)	20	48	28	3
As at 31 Aug 2011 (21,933)	20	50	29	2
As at 31 Aug 2010 (22,073)	18	50	30	3

Figure 8. Most recent overall effectiveness of schools over time[50]

49   Ibid.

50   Ofsted (2022) *State-funded schools inspections and outcomes as at 31 August 2022.* Available at: https://www.gov.uk/government/statistics/state-funded-schools-inspections-and-outcomes-as-at-31-august-2022/main-findings-state-funded-schools-inspections-and-outcomes-as-at-31-august-2022

Statistically there is no doubt that the number of schools which 'require improvement' has gone down: figure 8 shows 30% RI schools in 2010, down to 10% in 2022, while the number of 'good' and 'outstanding' schools has increased from 68% in 2010, to 88% in 2022. There have been some changes to the gradings in outstanding schools recently which has caused interest and upset, but school improvement as measured by Ofsted judgements has occurred.

However, like any single initiative in schools, it is very hard to prove single causation. Some of us will remember working in schools with specialisms where large sums of money came into our schools to develop that specialism. Then we had to provide annual proof of how this funding was responsible for the success of the entire school and we had to write evaluation reports demonstrating impact and value for money. Schools are way too complex to attribute impact to one single activity, strategy, initiative or approach to school improvement: it is always a combination of factors. It may be true that Ofsted frameworks help guide good practice, but so do many other things. Working with peer schools, having a strong leadership team, resilience and grit of staff, community buy-in... there are so many factors which all work together to make schools successful. Yes, schools have improved over time if we look at Ofsted judgements and their outcomes, but there is no research to say these improvements have occurred *because* of Ofsted.

In a paper prepared by Ofsted in 2010, the inspectorate made several claims about the impact of the inspection process on school improvement. Among their findings were the following:

- Independent evaluations have found that inspection has a significant impact on school improvement, especially in the weakest schools. Inspection can act as a catalyst for improvement and helps ensure schools are focusing on the right areas for development.
- The areas on which Ofsted focuses in inspection frameworks can help target improvement. For example, safeguarding arrangements have markedly improved since Ofsted introduced a more rigorous approach to this area.
- The National Foundation for Educational Research (NFER) evaluated Ofsted's impact between 2006 and 2009. The NFER emphasised the importance of classroom observation, high quality

feedback and clear, specific and straight-forward recommendations in published inspection reports. Teachers, in particular, reported that inspection helps identify where change is needed.

- Ofsted has an important role in driving improvement in the weakest schools. When a school is placed in 'special measures', for example, Ofsted holds a school improvement seminar with the headteacher, the governing body and a representative of the local authority to discuss the improvements needed. Ofsted inspectors then carry out monitoring visits of the schools, at a frequency of up to three visits a year, to support and check on progress.

- Since September 2005, 83% of schools improved sufficiently to have special measures removed by the time of their fifth monitoring visit. School leaders, teachers, and local authorities will have brought about the necessary improvements but headteachers of schools coming out of special measures say that Ofsted monitoring visits had a major impact. The Ofsted visits helped the school to focus on the right areas, kept the school on track, and imbued a rapid pace.[51]

Other more recent findings from 2022 show other evidence of improvement if we are looking at grades alone.

Out of the 1,600 graded inspections we carried out this academic year [1 September 2021 to 30 June 2022], nearly 600 were of schools previously judged to require improvement (RI).

A higher proportion of the RI schools inspected in 2021/22 have improved than in 2019/20: 70% compared with 56% in 2019/20.

A higher proportion of primary schools than secondary schools improved (71% compared with 68%). However, the biggest increase was for secondary schools, with an increase of 26 percentage points from 42% in 2019/20.[52]

---

51 Ofsted (2010) *The role and performance of Ofsted.* Memorandum submitted by Ofsted to the Commons Education Select Committee, October. Available at: https://publications.parliament.uk/pa/cm201011/cmselect/cmeduc/writev/ofsted/68.htm

52 Ofsted (2022) *Schools commentary July 2022: schools that require improvement.* Available at: https://www.gov.uk/government/publications/school-inspections-statistical-commentaries-2021-to-2022/schools-commentary-july-2022-schools-that-require-improvement

Inspection outcomes of previously RI primary schools, over time (percentages)

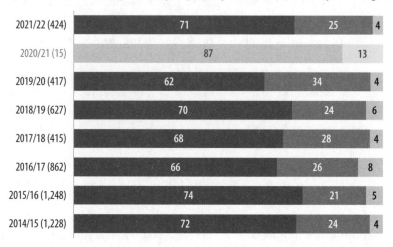

Figure 9. Inspection outcomes of previously RI primary schools, over time (percentages)[53]

However, we might disagree on what 'school improvement' actually means. No one would argue that we want a higher number of good and great schools in our system, but what is school improvement beyond a grade? Context is everything here. For one school it might be pupil numbers – going from undersubscribed to oversubscribed. For another it might be a reduction in the number of students who are designated as NEET (not in education, employment or training) when they leave the school. For many it will be outcomes, academically or with progress made by students.

---

53   Ibid.

Inspection outcomes of previously RI secondary schools, over time (percentages)

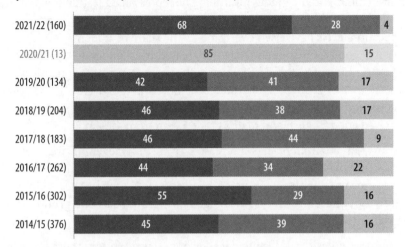

Figure 10. Inspection outcomes of previously RI secondary schools, over time (percentages)[54]

DOES OFSTED IMPROVE OUTCOMES?

How do we measure improvement? We could look at outcomes over time, examining attainment and test scores. We could look at progress measures over time, we could even look at our rankings in PISA tables. Like everything, improvement is subjective and context driven. We can see national pictures and make national and international comparisons, but what's really helpful and meaningful is to look at individual schools over time. And what about the learners themselves? What does school improvement look like for them? Have we improved the lives of the most disadvantaged in society, or those with special educational needs or disabilities, or those with protected characteristics?

---

54   Ibid.

Looking at attainment over time is difficult due to the changing nature of examinations and the grades awarded. The report on education inequalities in the Institute for Fiscal Studies Deaton Review series, notes that, 'Education levels have risen over time … the share of students achieving at least five good GCSEs or equivalent increased from under 40% in the early 1990s to a high of 82% in 2012. Even with the crossover of examinations we can see that in 1996, 35% of students achieved 5+ good GCSEs including English and maths, increasing to 57% in 2014, and in 2021, 48% of students achieved good English and maths grade 5+ up from 40% in 2017.'[55]

So, overall attainment has increased over time, even if we are not measuring like for like. This is positive and it might suggest that standards have improved because of Ofsted. However, let's look at the attainment figure for children from disadvantaged backgrounds as one group where gaps in attainment are not closing over time.

The report notes that, 'despite decades of policy attention, there has been virtually no change in the "disadvantage gap" in GCSE attainment over the past 20 years. While GCSE attainment has been increasing over time, 16-year-olds who are eligible for free school meals are still around 27 percentage points less likely to earn good GCSEs than less disadvantaged peers. Children from disadvantaged backgrounds also make slower progress through secondary school: in the 2019 GCSE cohort, just 40% of disadvantaged children who achieved the expected level at age 11 went on to earn good GCSEs in English and Maths, compared with 60% of their non-disadvantaged peers. And while virtually all (95%) of non-disadvantaged pupils who achieved above the expected level at age 11 went on to earn good GCSEs, one in six of primary school high achievers from disadvantaged backgrounds missed out on the GCSE benchmark.'

Might we say Ofsted is raising standards, but not for all?

The Education in England: Annual Report 2020, from the Education Policy Institute, found that, 'looked after children were 29 months behind other children,' and that 'gaps in attainment widened significantly over the past decade between Black Caribbean children/children from other black

---

55 Farquharson, C., McNally, S. and Tahir, I. (2022) *Education Inequalities. IFS Deaton Review of Inequalities.* Available at: https://ifs.org.uk/inequality/education-inequalities/

backgrounds, and children from other ethnicities.' These findings used figures from 2019, before the additional challenges of Covid. The report goes on to state that since 2011, 'there has been less progress in closing the gap for persistently disadvantaged pupils. More recently, increases in persistent poverty among disadvantaged pupils have contributed to the halt in progress for the wider disadvantaged group.'[56]

It was found that disadvantaged learners (see figure 11) were up to 22 months behind their peers and that other groups were also left behind.

	Early years	Primary school	Secondary school	
	EYFSP total point score	KS2 Scaled score in reading and maths	GCSE average grade	GCSE English and maths (average grade)
2011	-	10.6	20.4	19.7
2012	-	10.1	20.0	18.9
2013	4.7	10.0	19.6	18.6
2014	4.7	10.0	19.6	18.2
2015	4.6	9.7	19.4	18.1
2016	4.5	9.6	19.3	18.1
2017	4.5	9.5	18.4	17.9
2018	4.6	9.2	18.4	18.1
2019	4.6	9.3	18.4	18.1
2018-2019 change (%)	+0.1 (+1.4%)	+0.1 (+0.8%)	-0.0 (-0.2%)	+0.0 (+0.0%)
2011-2019 change (%)	n/a	-0.4 (-12.8%)	-2.0 (-9.8%)	-1.6 (-8.0%)

Figure 11. Trends in the size of the disadvantage gap since 2011[57]

The Education Policy Institute previously published the report *School Inspection in England: Is there room to improve?* in 2016, which found that, 'schools with more disadvantaged pupils are less likely to be judged "good" or "outstanding", while schools with low disadvantage and high prior attainment are much more likely to be rated highly:

---

56 Hutchinson, J., Reader, M. and Akhal, A. (2020) *The Education in England: Annual Report 2020*. Education Policy Institute. Available at: https://epi.org.uk/wp-content/uploads/2020/09/EPI_2020_Annual_Report_.pdf
57 Ibid.

- Secondary schools with up to 5% of pupils eligible for free school meals (FSM) are over three times as likely to be rated "outstanding" as schools with at least 23% FSM (48% compared with 14% "outstanding"). Those secondary schools with the most FSM pupils are much more likely to be rated 'inadequate' than those with the fewest (15% compared with 1%).

- For primary schools, those with high numbers of children on free school meals are still only half as likely as those with low proportions of pupils on free school meals to be judged outstanding (11% compared with 25%).

- The least deprived schools were also most likely to improve their Ofsted judgement and least likely to be down-graded, even after accounting for their previous Ofsted judgement.'[58]

Mary Bousted writes that, 'our education system compounds its deliberate neglect of poor children through the practices of Ofsted, an inspection agency that gives inaccurate and invalid inspection judgements that shame leaders and teachers working in schools with high levels of pupil deprivation.'[59]

In *So What Now?* Malcom Groves and John West-Burnham write about a 'flawed approach to accountability'. They reference statistics showing the level of child poverty in the UK where, 'children from Black and minority ethnic groups are more likely to be in poverty ... compared to children in White families.' While acknowledging that Ofsted may be beginning to show signs of understanding the associated significance of the socio-economic context of a school, the comparative judgements awarded by the inspectorate 'based on a simplistic homogeneity are no way to work towards challenging the lack of equity in the school system.'[60]

58 Hutchinson, J. (2016) *School Inspection in England: Is there room to improve?* Education Policy Institute. Available at: https://epi.org.uk/wp-content/uploads/2018/01/school-inspection-in-england-web.pdf

59 Bousted, M. (2022) *Support Not Surveillance*. Woodbridge: John Catt.

60 Groves, M. and West-Burnham, J. (2022) *So What Now? Time for learning in your school to face the future*. Woodbridge: John Catt.

Time and again we see that inspections and the current framework and even the thinking of some inspectors does not take context into account and does not reward schools that are working hard to close gaps, even when the odds are stacked against them. In some contexts, just managing to keep outcomes the same is not seen as doing a good job, even though the challenges are so great that it would be no surprise if standards were falling. Many people I speak to still mourn the loss of 'contextual value added' and while opponents say it lowered expectations and therefore standards, it did at least show an understanding of context.

In a 2022 blog, Ross McGill writes on whether inspection leads to school improvement.[61] He cites that in a 2012 paper, *The effect of school inspections: a systematic review*, improvement (following an inspection) may be defined as one or more of the following:

1. School improvement.
2. Behavioural change of teachers.
3. Student achievement results.

Additionally, he quotes from the review that, 'no evidence has been found that school inspections automatically lead to the improvement of the educational quality.' He does however note that the review reveals there is evidence that, 'a positive role is reserved for one aspect of regulative measures, namely feedback: the verbal feedback at the end of the inspection visit and also the written feedback in the inspection report.'[62]

DOES OFSTED OFFER VALUE FOR MONEY?

The National Audit Office reports on whether Ofsted's approach to inspecting schools is providing value for money. In their 2018 report it found that only 29% (£44 million) of its total (£151 million) spending went on inspecting state-funded schools in 2017-18, equivalent to 0.11%

---

61 McGill, R. M. (2022) Ofsted is not effective in driving school improvement. Blog post. *Teacher Toolkit.* Available at: https://www.teachertoolkit.co.uk/2022/07/31/ofsted-school-improvement/

62 Klerks, M. (2012) *The effect of school inspections: a systematic review.* Paper presented at the ORD, Wageningen, The Netherlands, June 20, 21 and 22. Available at: http://schoolinspections.eu/impact/wp-content/uploads/downloads/2013/12/ORD-paper-2012-Review-Effect-School-Inspections-MKLERKS.pdf

of the total funding for state-funded schools in the same year.[63] Some of the key points from the report, and my reactions to them, are listed below.

> *The system for school improvement and accountability is fragmented and there is some confusion about Ofsted's role. A range of different bodies are involved in holding schools to account and supporting them to improve, with different arrangements for maintained schools, academies and independent schools.*

All school leaders feel this breadth of pressure: governors, local authorities, MAT CEOs, as well as the inspectors themselves. I wrote in *School self-review – a sensible approach* about the pressure and workload issues of having to write several reports with the same detail in different formats for different groups. This could be much more streamlined and impactful by following some of the suggestions I put forward in chapter 8 of this book.

> *Ofsted does not decide what action should be taken after it has inspected a school and does not intervene to improve schools. These are matters for schools themselves, the Department, local authorities and multi-academy trusts. There is some overlap between the role of Ofsted and that of the Department's regional schools commissioners, who oversee academies' educational performance. The Department recognises the potential for confusion and duplication and, in May 2018, published principles for a clearer system of accountability.*

Having looked at these principles, I am none the wiser. How can Ofsted say it leads to school improvement when this report shows it does nothing to offer support and guidance after the inspections have been completed and the report is written?

> *Ofsted does not know whether its school inspections are having the intended impact: to raise the standards of education and improve the quality of children's and young people's lives.*

This, I feel, requires no comment.

---

63   National Audit Office (2018) *Ofsted's inspection of school.* Available at: https://www.nao.org.uk/wp-content/uploads/2018/05/Ofsteds-inspection-of-schools.pdf

Ofsted is one player in a complicated system so assessing the impact of school inspections is not straightforward but would be valuable.

Ofsted set few targets to measure performance against its 2016 strategic plan, and has provided limited information to allow others to assess its progress. Its performance measures have instead focused mainly on activity and processes.

It is difficult to see how these findings inspire confidence in Ofsted as an organisation.

In September 2017, Ofsted published a new strategy for 2017-2022. In March 2018, it agreed an evaluation framework for assessing performance against the strategy, including performance indicators and targets. The measures include the percentage of parents who consider that Ofsted is a valuable source of information, and the percentage of teachers who see Ofsted as a force for improvement.

While interesting, I don't really see how these are key performance indicators!

The report also states that 'until Ofsted has better information it will be unable to demonstrate that its inspection of schools represents value for money.'

None of this makes a convincing case that Ofsted offers value for public money, or that Ofsted inspections lead to school improvement.

CHAPTER 6
DEFENCE VERSUS CRITICISM

Ofsted's own categorisation of schools shows schools have improved, data over time has shown standards have risen for some but not for all, and some people like the Ofsted process more than others. So let's take a look at some of the key arguments for and against the current inspection regime.

In defence of Ofsted	Criticism of Ofsted
Parents use the grading system to give them an indication of school profile.	Ofsted practices impact negatively on health and well-being – Ofsted survey 2019.
Simplified grading system means it is easy for parents to understand.	Neutral or negative impact on student results – Teacher Support Network 2014.
Ofsted publishes school reports which are public and for all to see. Parents can look these up easily on the Ofsted website with a simple internet search.	Pressure on headteachers and leaders cascades down through the whole school community.
Ofsted does hold schools to account.	Some schools were seen to game the system, such as having students absent on inspection days / off rolling – Tyranny of metrics by Jerry Muller 2018.
Ofsted can show schools have improved over time.	Some schools have felt the pressure to deliver EBACC even if not necessarily the best offer for their students.
Inspections can show patterns within groups of student, subjects and national differences.	Inspectors may lack subject specific knowledge.
Ofsted demonstrates that they review the frameworks and adapt with feedback.	Judgements are like 'flipping a coin' – 2014 Policy Exchange think tank.
Inspection teams go through rigorous training so they understand the frameworks fully.	It has become increasingly hard to achieve / retain 'outstanding'.

Ofsted have awarded good grades to schools doing things differently (so it is possible) such as School XP.	The regular framework changes mean schools change their priorities according to Ofsted and not always their own needs.
Frameworks have seen the focus move from looking at data to focusing on intent and impact.	Current framework has caused an increase in workload with staff writing curriculum documents.
	The current framework has led to an obsession in some schools with mini-tests and rote learning to demonstrate knowledge has been 'learned'.
	Over emphasis on knowledge-rich curriculum – Prof Rose Luckin.
	Preparation for Ofsted takes time away from all school members, which could be spent doing something more meaningful, such as research.
	Schools have limited resources, especially small schools, to keep the website and all policies etc. up to date, despite wanting to.

Very few leaders would be against a fair accountability process. We are all professionals who are open to, and accepting of, critique and challenge. We hold ourselves and our teams to high standards and are happy to be held to account for this.

> *It's unfortunate that for many, Ofsted inspections remain a cause for high anxiety. However, if you're sufficiently well prepared, they can present an opportunity for you to really fly, and celebrate the successes of your students – particularly when the last two academic years are taken into account.*

Anthony David, executive headteacher[64]

There are so many published reports and surveys about Ofsted, and overwhelming consensus that Ofsted is no longer (if it ever was) fit for purpose. Ofsted have published their own findings about teachers' and leaders' views about inspections but there are many contradictory reports, increasing daily as I write.

---

64 David, A. (nd) School inspections for subject leaders – What is Ofsted looking for? Blog post. *Teachwire*. Available at: https://www.teachwire.net/news/school-inspections-for-subject-leaders-what-is-ofsted-looking-for/

Returning to the 2018 NAHT report, *Improving School Accountability*, the union sets out it owns criticism as shown below.

The current accountability system:

1. *Limits ambition. The high-stakes nature of inspection has helped to create a compliance culture in many schools which disincentivises innovation and can limit ambition. The inspection framework is too often treated as a tick-list to be measured against. Securing a 'good' or 'outstanding' judgement from Ofsted has become a goal in itself, rather than simply being seen as a snapshot description of where the school is on their journey to excellence. 'Outstanding' does not describe the pinnacle of educational excellence – if it did, arguably no-one should ever achieve it. Yet at present, there are few incentives to look beyond it.*

2. *Incentivises self-interest. The way in which we hold schools to account encourages self-interest over the good of the wider school community. There are few incentives for strong schools to lend their strength to those that are struggling, if by doing so it weakens them at their next inspection. Similarly, the over-reliance on pupil performance data to judge school effectiveness means there is little system incentive to put the interest of children with more complex needs first, for example in admissions or exclusion decisions, when doing so might result in an apparent dip in performance. Thankfully, the school system consists overwhelmingly of highly ethical leaders doing the right thing, in the interests of all children. At times, our system requires leaders to be brave and courageous in order to do the right thing for young people in the communities they serve. This needs to change so that doing the right thing is also the easiest thing to do.*

3. *Deters talented staff from working in more deprived communities. School leaders and teachers are put off teaching in schools serving more challenging communities because they do not believe they will be treated fairly by the inspectorate or performance tables. Research by the Education Policy Institute in 2016 found evidence to support this view and concluded "there is a clear and systematic negative correlation between school intakes with more disadvantaged children and more favourable Ofsted judgements". In other words, an inspection judgement can be as much a reflection of the area*

a school serves, as the quality of education provided within it. We will continue to struggle to close the attainment gap between pupils from poorer families and their more affluent peers unless we incentivise, not discourage, great people from working in the areas that need them most.

4. *Narrows the curriculum and encourages teaching to the test.* What is measured is valued. The nature and weight of the accountability system has encouraged schools to focus on those areas that are critical as school performance indicators, such as Key Stage 2 SATs, EBacc subjects or Progress 8. Despite the importance of an academic core, an over-emphasis has skewed and narrowed the curriculum. "Drilling" for SATs has become increasingly common, with some schools operating revision classes and practice tests during the school holidays to prepare eleven-year-olds for an assessment that is primarily designed to be a measure of school accountability. The use of narrow data in this way impedes a broader evaluation of the effectiveness of a school's curriculum in meeting the needs of the pupil cohort that it serves and the extent to which this prepares pupils for the future.

5. *Diverts attention from teaching and learning.* The value of a good inspection outcome and the fear of not being "Ofsted-ready" drives considerable activity in too many schools that could be better spent focused on improving teaching and learning. Tracking pupil progress and predicting outcomes have become an integral part of some schools to ensure they are prepared for Ofsted. The ability to show near real-time information on the progress of every pupil in a school, alongside predictions of future performance, has been interpreted as evidence of "leadership grip" by inspectors. Much of this analysis has been proven to have no validity or usefulness to teaching and learning. Too much time can be spent scrutinising data and too little on the leadership of learning. Moreover, the need to be "Ofsted-ready" and have evidence prepared creates significant workload burdens.

6. *Drives good people from the profession.* Fear, or the impact, of inspection is regularly recorded as a significant factor behind head teachers choosing to leave the profession prematurely, as well as influencing middle leaders not to progress to senior roles.

School leaders recognise the risk of leading a school which may be "downgraded" by Ofsted, seeing this as a personal, high-stakes risk which is likely to have a long-lasting impact on their career. Head teachers report their reaction to dropping a grade as being one of panic and vulnerability and the pressure of accountability is felt by leaders of schools, regardless of grade. Head teachers also say that too often they are held to account before they have the opportunity to make an impact. Likewise, the result of not hitting the mark in the latest annual round of primary tests or public examinations, has been shown to be a major driver of stress and anxiety, which is far from conducive to improvement.

7. *Provides less assurance of standards. The inspectorate provides much less independent assurance about the quality of education provided by individual schools than was previously the case. Ofsted no longer has the capacity or resources to inspect schools in any real depth. Even a "full" inspection only lasts for two days and this means that inspectors have to make significant, complex judgements about a school in a very short space of time with limited evidence to draw on. It is harder to make reliable and valid judgements about the quality of teaching in a school when often inspectors only have a few hours in which to do so.*[65]

Like many voices this report raises the issues of schools working towards Ofsted outcomes, which are not necessarily outcomes relevant to their children. It sets up schools against each other, making schooling a competitive endeavour. There is also concern raised about the focus on being Ofsted ready rather than prioritising what happens in the classroom. It puts staff off working in challenging schools – a factor I have personally experienced. I have witnessed headteachers shortlist by teachers working only in 'outstanding' schools as only they will know how to cope in their 'outstanding' schools. School leaders pass over application forms from staff working in 'requires improvement' schools because they 'must be bad themselves'. I have heard staff say that in the feedback they received after being rejected, one of the factors was that they didn't currently work in a good or outstanding school, somehow suggesting they themselves were a

---

65 NAHT (2018) *Improving School Accountability. Report of the NAHT Accountability Commission.* Available at: https://www.naht.org.uk/Portals/0/PDF's/Improving%20school%20accountability.pdf?ver=2021-04-27-121950-093/

poor teacher or leader. What irony, when so many struggling schools have excellent staff, which is why they are still coping.

Nicola Woolcock, writing for *The Times* in 2022, reports that, 'fewer than one in ten teachers think Ofsted has raised standards at their school.' She notes that while 'Amanda Spielman, the chief inspector, said recently that schools overwhelmingly found Ofsted inspections to be fair and constructive' and that, 'the vast majority said they would rate the regulator as "inadequate" or "requires improvement" and that they had no confidence in the current inspection system.' The article referred to a *Teacher Tapp* poll of about 5,000 teachers, carried out by The Times Education Commission, which found 'overwhelming levels of unhappiness with the watchdog', along with other worrying findings. For example, when respondents were asked if Ofsted had improved education at their school, 'just 1 per cent strongly agreed and 8 per cent agreed that it had. Thirty-two per cent disagreed and 27 per cent strongly disagreed, with the remainder unsure or unable to answer'.

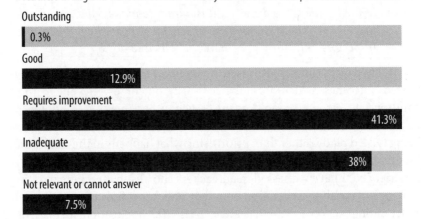

Rating Ofsted

Teachers in England were asked: How would you rate the overall performance of Ofsted?

Outstanding
0.3%

Good
12.9%

Requires improvement
41.3%

Inadequate
38%

Not relevant or cannot answer
7.5%

Survey respondents were 4,888 teachers in non-private schools in England
Source: Teacher Tapp

Figure 12. The views of nearly 5000 teachers when asked 'How would you rate the overall performance of Ofsted?'[66]

66 Woolcock, N. (2022) Teachers rate Ofsted 'inadequate', report finds. *The Times*. 22 June. Available at: https://www.thetimes.co.uk/article/teachers-rate-ofsted-inadequate-times-education-commission-k28l752ns

In contrast to Ofsted's own findings about teacher satisfaction with the inspectorate this survey found, 'no teachers said they strongly agreed that they had confidence in Ofsted, with 8 per cent agreeing, 32 per cent disagreeing and 32 per cent strongly disagreeing.'

Adrian Gray suggests 'It is clear that inspection can both evaluate schools and contribute to their improvement if the right conditions are met'. I interpret these 'right conditions' as having a framework of accountability but with the removal of the 'judgement' so that this contribution to improvement can be delivered. Gray is writing about inspectorates across Europe and makes some significant points: 'In general, inspectors do not provide on-going advice on making (these) improvements, as they do not have line management responsibility ... but they can comment on progress.'[67] This highlights the mixed messages we get with the English system: is Ofsted here to improve schools or here to judge?

As I write I find it increasingly contradictory that Ofsted tells us what 'good' looks like according to their own limited research base and makes judgements about us according to that research. Sometimes their own research ends up as an improvement point in a school inspection report and sometimes the school itself gives inspectors their own improvement points through their self-evaluation and conversations with inspectors. School reports then tend to offer three or four points on how to improve the school. But considering everything that is happening in the school, will just three or four short bullet points on what the school needs to do to improve really make a difference? Judge the school to be effective or not but leave the improvement strategy and planning to the school and its community of supportive professionals with the agency to help as necessary.

We know of course that total autonomy without accountability will not lead to school improvement, so we need a system where brokered support picks up on our improvement areas through our own detailed SEF (perhaps audited by Ofsted) and such partnerships create the improvement agenda together.

Meena Kemari Wood and Adrian Lyons, both former HMIs, share their thoughts regarding the changing Ofsted regime in an article for *Schools Week*. They write about their changing views and experiences of Ofsted

---

67   Gray, A. (2019) *European School Inspection and Evaluation*. Nottingham: Bookworm of Retford.

over time, and how they feel that 'Ofsted's role has shifted from aiming to improve lives by raising standards in education and children's social care' to a 'high-stakes, low-trust culture of school judgement'. Of the current framework they write, 'the framework itself is driven by an ideology of knowledge-rich curriculum, an obsession with cognitive science and reductive government targets for "academic EBacc subjects".

Their thoughts about the shifts towards the focus on curriculum in the framework are scathing. 'The engine room for the implementation of this policy is Ofsted's "curriculum unit" – a small group of mostly externally recruited HMI with minimal inspection or senior leadership experience. Their chief tool is the "subject deep dive", said to "provide evidence of curriculum quality, which informs our quality of education judgement". They think that the outcome of this is that schools match their curriculums to the framework and not necessarily consider what might work best for their own students. They appreciate the curriculum is important, but they say that, 'Ofsted's narrow curriculum for schools has failed. Implementation is inconsistent and the impact of reports does not capture learning. It is all about the intent; a school's ability to jump through Ofsted's curriculum hoops! It's time to place learners at the heart of the curriculum; to remove expectations of what schools should teach and how, and to confer professionalism back to the sector.'

Wood and Lyons are also unimpressed by the final reports inspectors write, calling them, 'anodyne, bland reports that do not capture the essence of their individual contexts. Prescribed stock phrases mean reports could be about any school, anywhere. It's dispiriting for school leaders, and the absence of any sense of local character means headteachers simply focus on the grade.'[68]

In his 2022 blog post, *What did Ofsted want schools to improve in 2021-2022?*, Peter Foster looked at over seventy inspection reports from September 2012 to September 2022, across all phases, and produced a summary of what schools with different judgments needed to work on. Worryingly he wonders, 'if the patterns or themes noticed here are an accurate reflection of the priorities of schools or if Ofsted are a homogenising force, making schools similar but not necessarily better. I'm not claiming schools must

68 Wood, M. K. and Lyons, A. (2022) Ofsted's autocratic curriculum experiment has failed. *Schools Week*. 3 August. Available at: https://schoolsweek.co.uk/ofsteds-autocratic-curriculum-experiment-has-failed/

improve the following things, simply that Ofsted made much of these things last year.' I have taken some of the key findings and put them into table form, then highlighted what I see as significant features and added some of my own thoughts in response to these.[69]

Areas for development across reports read		Comment
Outstanding	'Outstanding schools often get no areas for development. There are vague comments about *slight* inconsistencies in the curriculum or student behaviour but, as you'd expect, little else.'	Really? Nothing to improve?
Good	'In Good schools, over half the reports' areas for development focused on the sequence, ambition and planning of the *curriculum*.'	
Good - Primary	'In Primary, the overwhelming curriculum focus was on foundation subjects. Firstly, teachers' subject knowledge of foundation subjects is – quite understandably – less strong than in other areas of the curriculum. We could, of course, debate the fairness of expecting a primary teacher to know deeply about everything from music to science to history but time after time teacher knowledge is coming up as an area for *development*.'	This will be of no surprise to any primary school teacher or leader.
	'Parallel to the point about teacher knowledge is one about the lack of definition in the curriculum, particularly in foundation subjects. Teachers can't know what hasn't been defined. Again, the expectation on primary schools is perhaps unfair but the area for develop[ment] is consistent across schools. Definition is an area that comes up time and again. To be clear, the reports never mandate a particular scheme of work, mode or format for curriculum codification. But they frequently find that schools or leaders aren't clear enough about *what* will be taught.'	In my experience, inspectors have liked the teaching of an 'off the shelf' programme for some foundation subjects like PE, RS and PSHE, maybe this will be the way forward for science and humanities too.
	'Leaders don't monitor teaching and learning. Teachers don't have a clear grasp of the evidence. Leaders don't analyse the attendance to after school clubs (maybe they were too busy defining knowledge in foundation subjects).'	

69 Foster, P. (2022) *What did Ofsted want schools to improve in 2021-2022?* Blog post. Available at: https://curriculumteamleader.wordpress.com/2022/09/06/what-did-ofsted-want-schools-to-improve-in-2021-2022/

Good – Secondary	'In Secondary, curriculum featured just as much as an area for development. Often, the problem – as Ofsted see it – is that the curriculum is not ambitious enough. This *may* mean a school is still trying to get away with a three-year KS4. It may mean subjects aren't covered in sufficient depth. It may mean that KS3 isn't challenging enough.'	It is so hard to articulate what an ambitious curriculum is for all. Schools work hard to do this for their own context.
Good – both	'Curriculum features in some common ways across primary and secondary. Firstly, the curriculum doesn't define the knowledge which students need to learn (as mentioned above). Secondly, the curriculum isn't well sequenced and doesn't build on what students have learned previously. Thirdly, teaching doesn't assess the precise knowledge students must learn. This last point came up far more than I thought. Perhaps work on assessment hasn't caught up with curriculum development.'	I struggle to see how inspectors can make this judgement over a two-day visit.
	'The biggest area for development not curriculum related was around schools' provision for students with SEND. Often, teachers don't have the information they need about certain students or aren't acting on this information.'	The problem here is a national issue about schools having limited resources – all schools want to support learners with SEND – but too often do not have enough funding to do so.

In *Quality Assurance Processes: Ofsted Lecture,* the writers at UKEssays. com collated a range of thoughts about the strengths and limitations of the Ofsted inspection model. The article makes the following interesting points:

- 'The inspection model is open to critique, and the importance of inspection placed upon educators can be stressful and demoralising, as well as arguably fostering school environments which are tailored as much to the satisfaction of Ofsted inspection criteria as they are to meaningful learning and fostering of young people's education and growth.

- A generalised concern about Ofsted can result in safe and dependable, though unambitious and sterile teaching, and school environments designed as much to tick boxes as to inspire learners.

- Inspections are inevitably subjective to some extent; though there are safeguards within the model to mitigate against wayward grades, there is nevertheless an element of inconsistency and, at times, inaccuracy in grading, reporting, and in the application of Ofsted guidelines to settings.'

In defence of Ofsted the report argues:

- 'A removal of Ofsted would mean that school performance measures would default to an over-analysis and reliance on test scores, which can have a series of interlinked negatives associated with such a regime. These include teaching to test, rote-based learning in the young, and narrowing of curricula and of teaching methods as exam-friendly criteria and topic areas become the focus of instruction.

- Europe-wide research indicates that school inspections have a positive impact on learner outcomes.

- Inspection programmes can also highlight good practice and help disseminate innovation when it is found.

- Since its inception, Ofsted has increased the accountability of school and individual educators, has improved the transparency of the education system, and its grading has been found to be useful to parents.'

They continue to comment that although there are positives they found that some people feel Ofsted is, 'insufficiently flexible to take into full account the contexts of education; the school is the focus, and not necessarily the ways in which the school must manage its intake, and the social and cultural issues associated with that pupil body. This can mean that schools in areas of low economic performance – where there are issues with poverty, with high proportions of learners for whom English is not a first language, and/or where there are other social deprivation indices at play – can be held perhaps unfairly accountable for the consequences of contexts which they are not responsible for.'[70]

---

70 Essays, UK. (November 2018) *Quality Assurance Processes – Ofsted Lecture*. Available at: https://www.ukessays.com/lectures/education/best-practice/qa/?vref=1

Writing in *Tribune*, Robert Poole and Daniel Whittall claim that 'Ofsted has spent its thirty years inflicting surveillance and stress on teachers and judging working-class schools more harshly than their wealthy counterparts – it must be replaced … In 2017, however, the National Audit Office concluded that Ofsted "does not know whether its school inspections are having the intended impact: to raise the standards of education and improve the quality of children's and young people's lives."'

They quote the DfE's 2019 review *School improvement systems in high performing countries* which notes that in Germany, they '"operate low-stakes systems, with inspection results not generally published", and that internationally the most effective education systems "place a strong emphasis on school-to-school collaboration and peer-to-peer support". And they call for a new system, favouring local collaboration where teachers are, 'supported to be their best, one in which our professionalism is respected and valued, and one in which – most importantly – pupils are treated equally and not disadvantaged due to their class position.'[71]

Helena McVeigh writes that, 'performativity is a response to the accountability regime that schools now find themselves in, with the outcomes of an Ofsted inspection becoming increasingly high stakes.' She notes that some school leaders have 'slavishly' followed the Ofsted handbook instead of using it as a guide, and that they have begun to 'emulate some of the inspection practices in their own schools'. She discusses practices we all recognise and which some of us have been responsible for such as 'deep dives', whereby some staff 'are under permanent scrutiny by their own senior leaders'.[72]

A 2022 *Schools Week* article confirms the inconsistent approach that Ofsted has taken in the past; and although it now says it is remedying matters, this has led to different pressures in the system. The results of inspections of 'outstanding' schools which had been exempt from 2010-2020 caused upset among school leaders and communities, when 'more than four-fifths of "outstanding" schools inspected last year lost their

---

71   Poole, R. and Whittall, D. (2022) How Ofsted undermines our education system. *Tribune*. 6 May. Available at: https://tribunemag.co.uk/2022/05/ofsted-schools-teachers-education-inspection-neu

72   McVeigh, H. (2020) *Teaching and the role of Ofsted*. London: UCL-IOE press.

coveted top grade'. It was reported that 'the majority (62%) became "good", but over a fifth fell to "requires improvement" (17%) or "inadequate" (4%)'. Some of these schools had not been inspected for 15 years![73]

WHAT ABOUT THE INSPECTORS THEMSELVES?

'Inconsistency of inspectors' comes up time and again as a real concern. People talk about their Ofsted experiences and compare the process and the attitudes of the inspection team itself, especially the lead inspector. Some teams have been described as authoritarian rather than authoritative. Sometimes the lead inspector is a His Majesty's Inspector (HMI) which, in my experience, people tend to appreciate more, but some are not.

There are questions around the experience of inspectors; obviously some are new, and some not so new, but all will have gone through a rigorous recruitment process and will have had extensive training. There have been questions raised about inspectors being experienced but not being able to lead their team well. Issues also arise when inspectors have not had any or enough experience in the educational phase or setting they are inspecting. Dynamics are everything here and we might all agree that effective teams work well together and know each other well, but not all inspection teams will have met before they are put together on the day of the visit. It seems we don't, and may never have, total consistency here, and this really is a big concern. We might say we need objectivity but get subjectivity, but actually maybe we need subjectivity when it comes to things like understanding that schools are in different contexts.

Mc Veigh writes in *Teaching and the Role of Ofsted: An investigation*, that: 'the way headteachers respond to an inspection has, in my experience, been critical in setting the tone for the way that teachers respond to the process.' She adds that another issue is when headteachers may try to 'second guess Ofsted expectations' as it is not often 'clear whether two

---

73   Whittaker, F. (2022) Four in five 'outstanding' schools lose top Ofsted grade. *Schools Week*. 22 November. Available at: https://schoolsweek.co.uk/four-in-five-outstanding-schools-lose-top-ofsted-grade/?utm_content=bufferb621a&utm_medium=social&utm_source=linkedin.com&utm_campaign=buffer

different inspectors would arrive at the same judgement'. She cites a report by the Education Committee which found that there was variable quality in inspection teams. From her own experiences she writes 'team inspectors often have their own preferred views about, for example, what is best practice in teaching children in early years'.[74]

The 2023 paper *Are some school inspectors more lenient than others?* presents evidence drawn from the data of more than 30,000 school inspections conducted in England between 2011 and 2019.

One of the key findings was that:

> *Male inspectors are found to award slightly more lenient judgements to primary schools than their female counterparts, while permanent Ofsted employees (Her Majesty's Inspectors) are found to be harsher than those who inspect schools on a freelance basis (Ofsted Inspectors).*

The report also looked into who can be an inspector and found two types of appointees:

- *The first are Her [His] Majesty's Inspectors (HMIs). These individuals are permanent, usually full-time Ofsted employees. They are employed as civil servants and work for Ofsted as their only job.*

- *The second category are Ofsted Inspectors (OIs). These individuals work for Ofsted as freelancers and conduct inspections on an ad-hoc basis. OIs typically hold other jobs, with many being education professionals working in schools (e.g. as headteachers or other senior school leaders). Up until September 2015, OIs were employed by private sector organisations such as Serco. They have however since been directly contracted by Ofsted. This led to a sharp decline in the number of OIs – from around 3,000 to 1,600.*

---

74   McVeigh, H. (2020) *Teaching and the role of Ofsted*. London: UCL-IOE press.

The research paper asks a number of research questions which are relevant to this book, as shown below.

RQ2. Do female inspectors make harsher or more lenient judgements about schools than their male counterparts?
RQ3. Do Ofsted inspection judgements differ between OIs and HMIs?
RQ4. How are inspection outcomes linked to inspection experience of lead inspectors?
RQ5. Do inspectors judge schools more harshly when they are working outside of their home region?
RQ6. Do inspectors with a specialism in secondary school inspections judge primary schools more harshly than inspectors with a primary specialism?
RQ7. Do school inspection outcomes vary by inspection team size? Do outcomes differ between team versus individual inspections?

This study was one of the first of its kind and the conclusions demonstrate clearly the inconsistency of inspectors with regards to Ofsted outcomes.

- *Male inspectors make more lenient judgements about primary schools than female lead inspectors – particularly pronounced at the highest stakes (Inadequate) grade.*

- *Much larger differences are observed between inspectors working under different contractual arrangements (HMIs versus OIs), with the former consistently reaching harsher judgements than the latter, even after controlling for a wide array of school and inspection characteristics.*

- *Inspection team size also appears to be independently associated with inspection outcomes, most notably with inspections being conducted by a single individual being less likely to lead to a negative outcome (and more likely to award the modal Good grade) than a team of two inspectors or more.*

- *Little association was found between inspection outcomes and the lead inspector's experience, primary/secondary specialism or whether the inspection was conducted outside their home region.*

- *Variation in judgements across inspectors may be greater now than under previous frameworks, given the move towards inspectors making professional judgements about curriculum quality, with less emphasis put upon more objective national examination data.*

The report also suggests that school inspectorates should publish more research into the reliability and consistency of inspections, including variation in inspection outcomes.[75]

So who should be an inspector? Adrian Gray's research shows a few differences between countries, with some requiring inspectors to have a number of years' experience as a school leader, or pass an exam, or indeed both, as is the case in Belgium where a formal qualification and a minimum of seven years' experience is needed. Gray notes that in 2011 'a Parliamentary committee in England complained that too few inspectors in England had recent school experience' and that from 2014, 'Ofsted increasingly sought to recruit serving school leaders as inspectors in order to win the confidence of the profession.' He noted that, 'there are two concerns here – how many serving inspectors come from schools facing challenging circumstances since you couldn't be an inspector if you were working in a RI or inadequate school, opposed to the number coming from outstanding schools in "outstanding areas".' The other concern is the 'divisive nature of the advantage to some schools of having a school leader who is also an inspector having the inside knowledge of what the Inspectorate is looking for and judging.'[76]

WHAT ABOUT THE FRAMEWORK ITSELF?

The 2019 framework and the subsequent changes in the 2022 update have led, in some cases, to an absolute focus on memory as if this is the end goal of education: 'Children should know more and do more.' Of course! Of course a learner's journey through school should mean they know more and do more, but being heavily focused on this can get a bit extreme at times. We have all heard stories of inspectors asking children, some as young as four, about what they learned yesterday or last week or at the start of the term. If I ask my teenager what she had for lunch she won't often remember. Of course, we need to develop strategies to help learners remember and help shift information from short-term to long-

75   Bokhove, C., Jerrim, J. and Sims, S. (2023) *Are some school inspectors more lenient than others?* University of Southampton. Available at: https://eprints.soton.ac.uk/473908/1/WP_Inspector_Effects_FINAL_020223.pdf

76   Gray, A. (2019) *European School Inspection and Evaluation*. Nottingham: Bookworm of Retford.

term memories, yes there are specific strategies that make this process more efficient and yes, as a workforce we are all striving to do this daily. However, to 'test' this by asking on the spot questions doesn't seem the best way to understand if our efforts are working. What teacher talked about schema before 2019? We have always known what this means, maybe without labelling it as such, and we continuously work on developing this in our learners, but the obsession with the term has become a bit farcical. Not to sound like one of those teachers who has been there and done it all, but we have always thought about the big picture, starting points, end points and misconceptions. I am not criticising the current framework for its focus on this at all, but I am sceptical about the occasional implication that this is all new. The release of Ofsted crib sheets on social media in 2022 really brought this to the fore. There was quite a furore caused by the knowledge that inspectors who are serving headteachers are 'in the know' about the contents of the crib sheets, while their non-inspector counterparts are not. Ofsted were unhelpfully quiet about these crib sheets which didn't allay people's fears very much, adding to the view that inspections are inconsistent. However, with Ofsted Chief Inspectors regularly changing, frameworks also change, so we will just have to wait until the next one (probably in 2024) to see what the emphasis is and what new, or old, language we will need to converse in, and what training we will need to swiftly implement for our middle leaders.

WHO DECIDES WHAT GOOD QUALITY OF TEACHING AND LEARNING LOOKS LIKE?

Towards the end of this book, I call for an opportunity for the framework to be rewritten with much more input from a range of teams who have actually conducted high quality and credible research around what makes good teaching.

In *School self-review – a sensible approach* I wrote 'Ofsted (2019) states that, "Classroom practice, and in particular teaching effectiveness, is the single most important factor in school effectiveness. Teaching effectiveness is a strong predictor of pupils' progress throughout school, and having a succession of strong or weak teachers can have lasting effects."'[77] Thus it is

---

77   O'Brien, T. (2022) *School self-review – a sensible approach*. Woodbridge: John Catt.

of course imperative that we are able to make accurate judgements about the quality of teaching in our schools. We need a secure understanding of where good and great practice exists and a clear picture of where it doesn't so we can intervene, offer support and take steps to ensure students are not receiving poor quality teaching from practitioners who need this support to improve or are reluctant, or refuse, to work to improve. However, it is the 'how we know' that needs some discussion, and it is by discussing and agreeing on the mechanisms and tools we use to make professional judgments that we come to agree on what effective teaching looks like. What we then do with what we find leads to effective reviewing of teaching and learning.

What makes great teaching? Ofsted offer their own views on what effective teaching is in their overview of research papers.[78] In terms of being inspection ready and developing staff language around Ofsted views about teaching and learning, it is useful to share this with staff and governors.

However, who really knows best? In my last book I directed readers towards the report *What Makes Great Teaching* by Coe, Aloisi, Higgins and Elliot Major, who lay out six components as a starter kit for thinking about effective pedagogy:

- Pedagogical content knowledge
- Quality of instruction
- Classroom climate
- Classroom management
- Teacher beliefs
- Professional behaviours[79]

If we are to have an inspectorate and a framework against which we can benchmark our practice of teaching, then we must consult widely to establish best practice teaching and learning statements, and evidence about effective teaching and what it looks like in different contexts.

---

78 Ofsted (2019) *Education Inspection Framework; overview of research*. London: Ofsted.

79 Coe, R., Aloisi, C., Higgins, S. and Elliot Major, L. (2014). *What makes great teaching?* London: The Sutton Trust.

And we must draw on international research. The potential risk is that the framework is based on current political doctrine about what makes effective teaching. It leans heavily on the narrow view that our curriculum should be based on 'powerful knowledge' as prescribed by Hirsch and Young and advocated by Michael Gove. This narrow focus on memory has led to a whole industry of lesson starters, tools and mini quizzes being invented by teachers all over the country so that children can 'know more and do more'. No one would argue that we need knowledge, but we need a more holistic appreciation of what we do with this knowledge. I put together a presentation for staff at one school about memory and knowledge and stressed that surely it is what a learner does with any knowledge that is important.

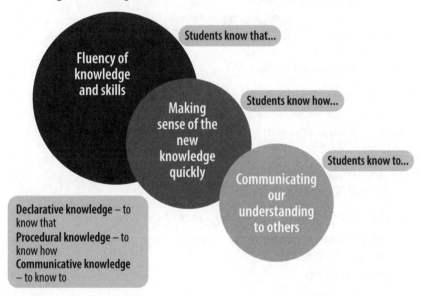

Figure 13. Memory and knowledge

I used the then trending language of declarative and procedural knowledge to develop a next step, which I called 'communicative knowledge' and it is this last idea which I don't think the current framework identifies as a skill.

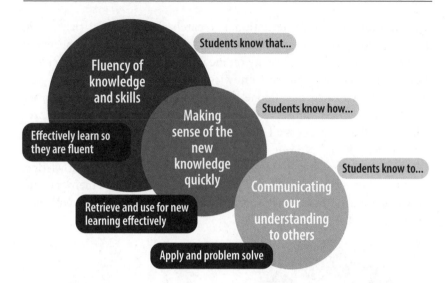

Figure 14. Communicative knowledge

The debate about knowledge versus skills still exists in some forums but I believe we can move on from this and acknowledge that of course we need knowledge, but it is ultimately what we do with this knowledge that should be valued.

McVeigh writes that the ways Ofsted promotes its views of good and effective teaching can be found in:

- the criteria in the inspection framework and handbooks
- supplementary guidance and case studies – though some of this activity has ceased
- survey reports
- annual reports
- blogs, twitter feeds (though these seem to have stopped)
- comments in individual school reports.[80]

I have seen the latter used in many schools as something to aspire to and used for training! Has anyone done this with their staff?

---

80   McVeigh, H. (2020) *Teaching and the role of Ofsted*. London: UCL-IOE press.

It is interesting to see, even with Ofsted, how the views around 'good teaching' in the Ofsted frameworks have changed over time; using the work of McVeigh I have noted a few of these changes.

Handbook date	Evaluation of teaching quality	Other comments	Possible implications
1994	Teachers have clear objectives for their lessons.	Inspectors should evaluate the marking of pupils' work.	All lessons had lesson objectives on the board and many students spent time copying these. Teachers marked a lot!
1999	How well the skills of literacy and numeracy are taught.	The extent to which teachers assess pupils' work thoroughly.	Teachers still marked a lot!
2005	Inspectors should evaluate the diagnosis of, and provision for, additional learning needs.	Learners are guided to assess their work themselves.	Teachers spent time developing success criteria and tried to enable students to self-assess. SENDCos became more important in schools and staff began to listen to their advice with some adaptations to lessons.
2015	Teachers make maximum use of lesson time. They use questioning highly effectively.		Pace became the word! CPD around questioning was everywhere.
2019	The school's curriculum intent and implementation are embedded securely. Teaching is designed so that pupils remember and can 'know more and do more'.		Middle leaders everywhere wrote curriculum statements for their subjects. Deep dives were invented. CPD around memory and cognitive load became the thing.

These changes have largely been welcomed in terms of the move away from obsessive marking, triple marking (though I was never sure what that was) and the three-part lesson. However, some changes have had too many unintended consequences. Our increasing understanding of memory and cognitive science is most welcomed, but the workload introduced around curriculum statements and deep dive preparation has been overwhelming. It is right that as teachers we should understand how the brain works and use this to inform our practice, which is why an engagement with a broad evidence base is essential in ensuring any inspection framework is not led by current political thinking and trends.

The move to not grading lessons was also welcomed by many, and as McVeigh found from experience as an inspector, 'at first, I welcomed the introduction of these grade descriptions, as I felt it would be easier to distinguish between the grades when judging the quality of teaching. In hindsight, this attempt by Ofsted to define outstanding, good, satisfactory and inadequate teaching was fraught with difficulty.'[81] I remember in one inspection my observed lessons were all on the same day and I was awarded a grade 1, 2 and 3 by the same inspector!

In the latest framework, Ofsted say they don't focus on outcomes and will not look at data, but school data is already out there on the DfE site. I know Ofsted look at this, they'd be daft not to. Financial details are also available on the DfE website, past Ofsted reports are online, and data is often displayed on a school's own website. When judging 'impact' and 'leadership and management' of course inspectors would look at all these documents.

In his 2022 post on *LinkedIn*, Daniel Sobel gives his views on Ofsted and the effect it has on schools and the people in them.

> *The amble down research-lane has exposed not only the lack of supporting evidence for the approach of OFSTED but some serious flaws. However, the biggest piece I think is what it is doing to the system of education. This is where we may split in our views as we begin to tread onto the rocky terrain of the political. However, I have tried to simply demonstrate that the research suggests that our education system is being inhibited by the OFSTED phenomenon and if we were to 'OFSTED' OFSTED against their core aim to up standards of education in England, we might find that they would get, I don't know, say 'embarrassingly inadequate'.*

---

81 Ibid.

He continues, noting that:

OFSTED equivalents exist in nearly all countries; they have played a key role in the development of public education systems, by monitoring the quality of schools and by supporting their improvement. However, in many countries, including England, these services are under increasingly heavy critique, because of their failure to have a positive impact on the quality of teaching and learning (De Grauwe & Carron, 2011). To improve educational quality, many countries have attempted to reform their supervision (inspection) systems.

Sobel calls for teacher professionalism to be recognised in this system of school evaluation.

A professional accountability model can provide an answer to the problem of classical state control in education supervision such as OFSTED. In this model, the main focus is not with the bureaucracy but the professional community – in our case, the teaching staff. They are supposed to be the best judges of how to ensure quality education (De Grauwe & Carron, 2011). As per one of the key arguments, the stronger the professional autonomy of teachers and schools, the more responsive they will be to the needs and conditions of their clients. Professional accountability protects schools against excessive external pressure, for example to boost school results. The legitimacy of this model derives from the expertise and ethical code of the teaching profession. Its dominant procedures of monitoring will be internal ones, such as self-evaluation by teachers and peer reviewing. Experience has shown that when teachers feel that control and support efforts all converge on the improvement of their classroom performance and when they are active partners in their own professional development, such efforts have the greatest chances of success.

His closing passage draws comparisons with the Finnish model and offers alternatives to the current Ofsted framework.

A country that has gone a long way in shifting towards a professional accountability system is Finland, where the external inspection model was abolished in 1991 (De Grauwe & Carron, 2011); an OECD report from 2020 notes Finland's 'strong tradition of high educational outcomes... both students and teachers in Finland view schools as supportive environments... Finnish teachers feel valued in society and enjoy positive working conditions' and, importantly, there is 'a strong improvement-focused evaluation culture in place in Finland, which helps foster an accountability system based on local needs, professionalism and trust.' So, thinking beyond the constraints of the antiquated OFSTED model, something like this might be a simple road map to a more meaningful, humane system:

- *Concentrate on the relationships between staff, students and home*
- *Give more professional authority to schools*
- *Use internal monitoring tools, like self-evaluations by teachers and peer reviewing which are premised on support not judgement*

In my career working with many schools around the country, I've seen distinct patterns and trends; one is that OFSTED reports are wholly unreliable and inconsistent. Headteacher colleagues and friends live in fear of the next inspection, which causes untold and unjustifiable stress.[82]

WHAT DO GOVERNORS SAY?

The 2022 report *School inspection: A view from the board, two years on* from the National Governance Association, aimed to consider whether schools are inspected in a consistent way under the latest Education Inspection Framework, whether governance is understood and inspected correctly, and whether the reporting of governance is consistent and achieves the intention of the reports that are published. The overall conclusions were that as a body, governors were not recognised or included as fully as they could be in the inspection process, and that, 'inspectors are not actively engaging with governors or trustees to a degree that satisfies the main aims and objectives of the schools inspectorate.'

The report contains some more interesting findings:

---

82   Sobel, D. (2022) Ofsted is inadequate. Blog post. *LinkedIn*. Available at: https://www.linkedin.com/pulse/ofsted-inadequate-daniel-sobel/

When inspecting governance, 'only 36% of governing boards said that the Ofsted inspection helped governance ... and fewer respondents in 2022 reported that inspectors did not understand the role of governance in the school and the line of questioning strayed into the operational function of the school.'

When inspecting to improve education, 'there is an inconsistency between the questions inspectors ask governing boards about the curriculum and the depth the questioning goes to. Despite the quality of education having the greatest weighting of all the judgement areas, governing boards are not always asked about their role in the curriculum and the depth of these conversations differ from school to school.'

When looking at the inspection process and reports, 'the role and impact of governance continues to be diminished from the reports with 31% of analysed reports not mentioning governance.'

The report shows the results of a survey of governors, who were asked about the extent to which their Ofsted inspection helped to improve governance (figure 15).

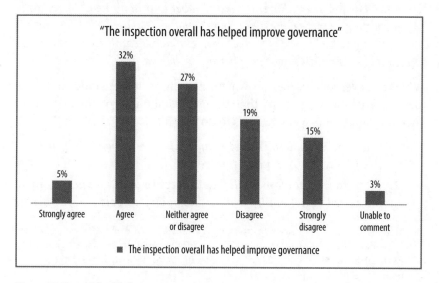

Figure 15. Does Ofsted help improve governance?

While figure 15 shows that while 37% of respondents felt the inspection had improved governance, a significant 27% felt unsure. Although many didn't feel they spent very long with the inspectors they did find they agreed with the inspection outcome.

The report asks that, 'Ofsted should ensure that as governance is a critical aspect of leadership which should be positively adding value to the school or trust's success or failure, this is both explored fully and recognised throughout the inspection process.'[83]

TO GRADE, OR NOT TO GRADE

People also have an issue with the grading itself, with many calling for Ofsted to dispense with the grades and maybe just write a report. Writing for *The Times* in his article 'Ofsted's culture of fear is bad for Britain's schools' Harry Hudson contends that:

> *The whole system of labelling schools with such blunt descriptors is deeply flawed and has turned Ofsted into little more than a Tripadvisor for schools. Worse still, an Ofsted rating is decided by one review and lasts for years. Parents see the label and don't need to read the inspection report, while a grading of good, in particular, covers such a multitude of schools as to have been rendered virtually meaningless. A simple pass or fail might be a better way forward.*[84]

While not everyone agrees on what a new inspectorate could look like, there is growing agreement that the grades should go. In 2018, Tom Sherrington listed five key reasons to do so.

1. *They are a ludicrous over-simplification – schools are just too complicated to sum up in this way.*

2. *Inspection is fundamentally too subjective and unreliable – there have been no reliability trials in secondary schools to test whether*

---

83   Sharma, N. (2022) *School inspection: A view from the board, two years on.* National Governance Association. Available at: https://www.nga.org.uk/getmedia/9dfdb398-0022-4b88-9ae8-c00f2f9b408a/nga-view-from-the-board-20220615.pdf

84   Hudson, H. (2022) Ofsted's culture of fear is bad for Britain's schools. *The Times.* 12 December. Available at: https://www.thetimes.co.uk/article/ofsteds-culture-of-fear-is-bad-for-britains-schools-qp5fnsb8j

different teams would arrive at similar judgements or would interpret observations and data in similar ways.

3. *The public interest illusion – in a totally direct and obvious way, the lower grades have the effect of shaming schools and their leaders. This makes it harder for them to do their work, not easier. How is this in the public interest? It just isn't.*

4. *The hideous hubris of 'outstanding' – and the albatross effect; I'll admit to finding the public big-ups around 'outstanding' judgements irritating.*

5. *Every School Requires Improvement – finally, isn't this just the most obvious thing; all schools require improvement. Wouldn't it just be so much better if we took all the labels off the reports, forced people to read them and left all schools with a record of their areas of strength and areas for development? Sure, we need a category for 'below the line' and a separate process for dealing with urgent safeguarding failures, but even here I would argue that it should be called something that suggested maximum support was on its way, recognising the challenges at work not the pejorative Jack Boots of 'inadequate' that just kicks everyone in the teeth.*[85]

Ben Newmark also worries about the impact of the grading system, writing that, 'varying levels of anxiety based on results is a useful way to focus our thinking; teachers are scared of Ofsted, not so much because of the process of inspection itself, but because they are afraid of a negative outcome; it is the judgements of "Requires Improvement" and "Inadequate" that are actually the real sources of fear.' He explains that this fear is related to what teachers and leaders worry might happen if the judgements are bad; he has little faith in the appeal system, and suggests that one outcome is that the headteacher may lose their job. He has found that, 'those in post for five years or more have only around a 20% chance of keeping their job three years after an "Inadequate" judgement. For those in position between two and four years, only around 40% will be still the Head three years after the bad report. Those appointed less than two years before the inspection,

---

85 Sherrington, T. (2018) Five reasons to ditch Ofsted grades. Blog post. *Teacherhead.* March 18. Available at: https://teacherhead.com/2018/03/14/five-reasons-to-ditch-ofsted-grades/

probably because they can better make the case that the school's failings aren't their fault, generally fare much better, with 80% still in place three years after inspection, which somewhat skews the overall figure of around a quarter moving on within three years.' No wonder that the fear is so real for headteachers.[86]

Nevertheless, supporters of the current system of inspection would argue that parents really do use Ofsted reports to help inform their decisions about where to send their child. I know of one parent who hadn't read a single actual report but was determined that her child could only go to an 'outstanding' school.

In defence of the current grading system, the 2019 Ofsted report *Retaining the current grading system in education* acknowledges that there have been criticisms of the grading system, as summarised below.

> *The arguments from commentators against the current system have been well rehearsed, so we will only summarise them here:*
>
> - *The current grading system has consequences that are seen by some to lead to an enormous amount of pressure on schools and headteachers. People feel that the high-stakes nature of accountability can have negative consequences in terms of provider behaviours (such as gaming league tables), health and well-being of staff and disincentivising collaboration with other providers. This is not just the case for providers in the bottom categories: some people argue that there is also a great deal of pressure on providers to maintain outstanding grades.*
> - *Outstanding schools are exempted from routine inspection by legislation* [since changed]. *Some outstanding schools have not been inspected for over 10 years. Their outstanding grade was obtained under a different inspection framework.*
>
>   *For this approach to work we must assume that those providers' effectiveness is stable, and that we can pick up declining standards through exam results or safeguarding reports. It is not clear that this is always true. This, however, is not so much*

---

86   Newmark, B. (2018) *Why are teachers so scared of Ofsted?* Blog post. Available at: https://bennewmark.wordpress.com/2018/06/09/why-are-teachers-so-scared-of-ofsted/

an argument for the grading system to be changed as for the exemption to be removed.

- *It can be challenging to provide grades for very large and complex further education and skills (FES) providers that are spread across a range of settings or regions.*

However, despite these concerns, they argue that these views are not persuasive enough to remove grades and instead set out their reasons for retaining the grading system:

- An effective system of school and provider choice requires information for parents.
- Parental trust in the current system is high.
- Teachers' trust in the current system is higher than often realised.
- Providing information for those seeking to improve standards.
- Inspection grades provide useful complementary information to policymakers.
- The grading structure underpins legislation.
- The four-point grading system as the best practice model.[87]

Ofsted argues that parents understand the grading system, and that they have found through their own surveys that parents largely trust Ofsted reports, although no questions directly relating to the grading system were asked. When commenting on teachers' perceptions, the report uses the results from the Ofsted commissioned 2018 YouGov poll *Teachers' awareness and perceptions of Ofsted* as shown in figure 16, which shows:

- 49% of teachers agreed that a clear grading system allows schools to know what they are aiming for and helps parents, while 34% disagreed.
- 40% stated a preference for an above/below the line system, with a significant minority (24%) disagreeing.

---

87 Ofsted (2019) *Retaining the current grading system in education. Some arguments and evidence.* Available at: https://assets.publishing.service.gov.uk/government/uploads/system/uploads/attachment_data/file/936220/Retaining_the_current_grading_system_-_arguments_and_evidence_290419.pdf

Almost half (48%) of teachers agree that a clear grading system allows schools to know what they are aiming for, and 40% say an above the line/below the line system would be better

- Ofsted currently gives schools an overall judgement grade of either, inadequate, requires improvement, good or outstanding. There is ongoing debate about the impact and desirability of this structure.

- Less experienced teachers are more likely to agree with this statement on the grading system than those more experienced teachers
  - 79% NQTs agree
  - 64% of 1-3 years experience agree
  - 51% of 4-6 years experience agree
  - 46% of 7-15 years experience agree
  - 39% of 16+ years experience agree

- Teachers aware of Ofsted's myth busting campaign are much more likely than those not aware of the campaign to disagree with this statement (54% v 33% disagree)
- 40% of teachers in outstanding schools agree with this statement

YouGov

	Strongly agree	Agree	Neither agree nor disagree	Disagree	Strongly disagree	Don't know
A clear grading system allows schools to know what they are aiming for and also helps parents readily understand the quality of education in a school	8%	41%	16%	23%	11%	29%
Moving to an above the line/below the line system would be better	9%	31%	27%	18%	6%	10%
The benefits for schools that reach outstanding are too important to take this judgment grade out of the structure	6%	24%	22%	28%	12%	8%

G1. Ofsted currently gives schools an overall judgement grade of either, inadequate, requires improvement, good or outstanding. To what extent do you agree or disagree with the following statements? Ofsted currently gives schools an overall judgement grade of either, inadequate, requires improvement, good or outstanding. There is ongoing debate with the following statements?

Figure 16. Teacher responses to questions around the Ofsted grading system[88]

88 YouGov (2018) *Teachers' awareness and perceptions of Ofsted Teacher Attitude Survey 2018 report.* Available at: https://assets.publishing.service.gov.uk/government/uploads/system/uploads/attachment_data/file/734327/Teachers_Attitude_Survey_2018_awareness_and_perceptions_of_Ofsted_Final_Report_August_2018.pdf

Furthermore, they argue that removing the grades would have unintended consequences:

- *Moving to a below/above the line system would make the decision to place a provider below the line potentially even more high stakes than the current good/requires improvement cut-off, because all the providers placed below the line would be in a single 'failed' category. More providers might become eligible for intervention of one sort or another.*

- *Not grading or moving to a below/above the line system could lead to the system becoming even more reliant on attainment or progress outcomes as the main measure. This in turn could increase behaviours such as off-rolling and gaming the exam system.*[89]

Amanda Spielman in 2023 wrote that, 'the broader debate about reforming inspections to remove grades is a legitimate one, but it shouldn't lose sight of how grades are currently used. They give parents a simple and accessible summary of a school's strengths and weaknesses. They are also now used to guide government decisions about when to intervene in struggling schools. Any changes to the current system would have to meet the needs both of parents and the government.'[90] This demonstrates that Ofsted are at least talking about grades.

What if we had a grade for each section, but no overall grade? This would encourage parents to look into the reports and maybe see grades for the areas which are most important to them, and what the school needs to do, or is doing, to improve. Some parents might place more value on outcomes, or personal development, or opportunities for enrichment.

Another advocate of removing grades is Caroline Derbyshire. In her blog post *However you read it, drop the Ofsted grades*, she writes that, 'the final thing to note is that grading only helped the school system to improve while it was expedient to expect "Outstanding" schools to do

---

89 Ofsted (2019) *Retaining the current grading system in education. Some arguments and evidence.* Available at: https://assets.publishing.service.gov.uk/government/uploads/system/uploads/attachment_data/file/936220/Retaining_the_current_grading_system_-_arguments_and_evidence_290419.pdf

90 Ofsted (2023) *Statement from His Majesty's Chief Inspector.* Available at: https://www.gov.uk/government/news/statement-from-his-majestys-chief-inspector

their community service by leading the system. There is no evidence that the grading helped those schools for their own sake. The fact that many are no longer seen to be as strong as they once were suggests that grading schools in no way helps to improve them.' She also worries about the consequences and implications of ungraded inspections:

> If only this 'ungraded' notion was genuinely the case. An ungraded inspection is very far from ungraded. There are four possible outcomes and all four of them are about grades:
>
> 1 – The school could get a letter to say that its current grade remains the same.
>
> 2 – It could be better than that and, horror of horrors, be given a more intensive inspection to determine whether it deserves such an accolade.
>
> 3 – It could be worse than it is and have a follow-up inspection to determine that. Can you imagine the misery of that kind of purgatory?
>
> 4 – The ungraded inspection is converted to a graded one because the school is inadequate in a key area such as safeguarding. Why wait four years to discover this?

She adds, 'absolutely everything about the so-called ungraded inspection is about grades. The system could be so much better, effective and kinder.'[91]

DOES THE CURRENT SYSTEM HELP PARENTS?

Often parents use the report as well as other indicators to help them get a sense of the characteristics and culture of the school. The Politics. co.uk website reports that, 'Supporters of the current arrangements point to the large degree of public support for the simple four point grading system operated by Ofsted.'[92] While the report of the 2021 *YouGov Parents Annual Survey* found, among other things:

- *Seven in ten (71%) parents feel Ofsted reports are a reliable source of information.*

---

91 Derbyshire, C, (2022) However you read it: Drop the Ofsted grades. Blog post. *Headteachers' Roundtable*. Available at: https://headteachersroundtable.wordpress. com/2022/11/24/however-you-read-it-drop-the-ofsted-grades/

92 Politics.co.uk (2023) *Ofsted*. Available at: https://www.politics.co.uk/reference/ ofsted/

- *The majority (60%) agree that Ofsted provides a valuable measure of childcare, however, this has declined since 2020 (65%).*

- *Agreement that Ofsted is a valuable source of information on education and works to improve education has remained stable since 2016.*

- *It remains that one third of parents agree that Ofsted acts independently of the government.*

- *Parents are favourable towards the four-point grading system, with two thirds (66%) agreeing it helps them to make decisions about their child's education.*[93]

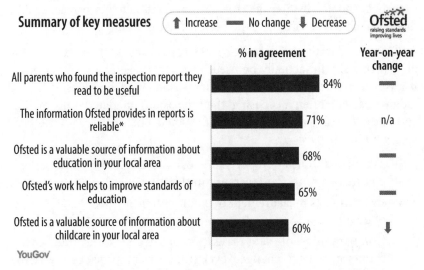

Figure 17. Summary of key measures in the Ofsted parents annual survey 2021[94]

In a 2020 article for *The Journal of Child Psychology and Psychiatry,* the authors ask, 'Why do parents look to Ofsted reports of schools?' They answer that it is because parents often believe in the Ofsted ratings index, but they 'could not find a single published study looking at the association between school-level Ofsted ratings and individual-level outcomes.' They also found that factors many parents cared about, such as wellbeing and achievement of students, are 'negligibly predicted by Ofsted ratings' and

93   Ofsted (2021) *Parents annual survey 2021.* Available at: https://assets.publishing. service.gov.uk/government/uploads/system/uploads/attachment_data/file/987970/ Ofsted_Parents_Annual_Survey_2021.pdf
94   Ibid.

that, 'Ofsted-rated school quality is a weak predictor of secondary school outcomes at age 16, including educational achievement, well-being and school engagement, once schools' student selection criteria have been taken into account.' Their findings, 'call into question the usefulness of Ofsted ratings as a guide for parents who are looking to make an informed choice for their children's secondary school.'[95]

However, Will Hazel, writing in *inews*, references a YouGov poll carried out for the University of Exeter, which shows that, 'almost two-thirds of parents don't consider Ofsted reports when deciding where to send their children to school. And nearly three quarters pay no attention to performance tables that rank schools according to their exam and test results.'[96]

A 2023 article in the *Journal of School Choice*, asks if Ofsted reports and judgements should actually be used by parents when choosing schools. It raises the issue that 'parents selecting secondary schools using Ofsted judgments will often be basing their decision on dated information,' and cites several reasons why parents should not solely rely on Ofsted information:

- Time-lag – Ofsted reports are backward looking, capturing a picture of a school at one point in time.

- Inspection as measurement of quality versus inspection as a driver of quality.

- Comparability of data – assessment frameworks and Ofsted frameworks have changed over time, so comparisons aren't like for like.

- The available choice set – parents only really choose between a few schools, often local to them.

- Added value over other information – parents often rely more heavily on other information such as word of mouth.

95 Stumm, S., Smith-Woolley, E., Cheesman, R., Pingault, J.-B., Asbury, K., Dale, P.S. et al. (2021) School quality ratings are weak predictors of students' achievement and well-being. *The Journal of Child Psychology and Psychiatry*, 62(3), 339-348. Available at: https://acamh.onlinelibrary.wiley.com/doi/10.1111/jcpp.13276

96 Hazel, W. (2021) Two-thirds of parents don't look at Ofsted inspection reports when choosing a school, poll finds. *Inews*. Available at: https://inews.co.uk/news/education/osfted-reports-inspection-ratings-parents-dont-care-choose-school-yougov-poll-1275609

Another significant consideration is that many parents don't really get to choose where their child goes to school. In bigger cities this may be relevant but in smaller towns and rural areas there really is little parental choice and so needing the grades for a school is less of an issue, but a report on key strengths and action points might be very informative.[97]

CAN OFSTED BE TRUSTED?

According to a *Teacher Tapp* blog in September 2022, which used data gathered from their own set of surveys, 'few of you have ever *strongly agreed* that Ofsted "acts as a reliable and trusted arbiter of standards across all different types of schools" and this year is similar to last. Although there was a brief high in 2019 (just after the introduction of the EIF) when 19% agreed, this dropped to 13% by 2021 and 12% this year. At the same time, strong disagreement is on the rise (up 4 percentage points since 2021, and 8 percentage points since 2019).'

'Ofsted acts as a reliable and trusted arbiter of standards across all different types of schools in England'

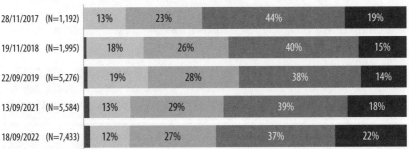

Teacher responses vary from 1,192 to 7,433 depending on date asked (results weighted to reflect national teacher and school demographics

■ Strongly agree   ▨ Neither agree nor disagree   ■ Strongly disagree
▨ Agree   ■ Disagree

Figure 18. Responses by year.

---

97   Bokhove, C., Jerrim, J. and Sims, S. (2023) How Useful are Ofsted Inspection judgements for Informing Secondary School Choice? *Journal of School Choice*, 17(1), 35-61. Available at: https://www.tandfonline.com/doi/full/10.1080/15582159 .2023.2169813

They found that more primary school respondents disagree or strongly disagree about the inspectorate's reliability.

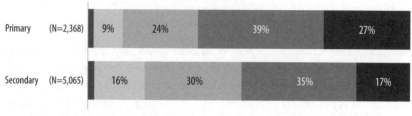

Figure 19. Responses by school type

And that opinions varied according to the last Ofsted grade awarded:

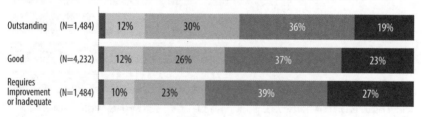

Figure 20. Responses by Ofsted grade[98]

98   Teacher Tapp (2022) Changing opinion on Ofsted, 'good lessons', deputies, and more. Blog post. *Teacher Tapp.* Available at: https://teachertapp.co.uk/articles/changing-opinion-on-ofsted-good-lessons-deputies-and-more/

An earlier blog from *Teacher Tapp* raised an interesting point in its title: Is Ofsted 'Reliable & Trusted'? It Depends How You Ask... They found that as people go through more Ofsteds, they become more cynical about its reliability and trustworthiness, that teachers in schools with the lower two grades were the least likely to say 'yes' their Ofsted was roughly accurate, and that 24% of teachers in 'outstanding' schools thought their grade overstated the quality of education provided. These findings and comments echo my thoughts in chapter 4. There are many factors which determine how people feel about Ofsted and inspections, and sometimes these change depending on one's own experiences.[99]

THE IMPACT OF POOR GRADES

In June 2022, *Headteacher Update* magazine reported on findings of the UCL report *'Stuck' schools: Can below good Ofsted inspections prevent sustainable improvement?*

> *The research, which has been funded by the Nuffield Foundation, classifies a stuck school as one that consistently received a less than good overall effectiveness inspection grade between 2005 and 2018 and for a minimum of three inspections.*

> *The report identifies a combination of 'unusually challenging circumstances' facing these schools including high teacher turnover, high pupil mobility, more disadvantaged pupils, being located in disadvantaged neighbourhoods, and higher levels of SEND.*

> *Many schools with lower Ofsted ratings can also find themselves undersubscribed, leading to less funding and therefore making improvement more difficult, especially in terms of hiring staff.*

The article continues:

> *A concerning finding in the report is that after receiving an initial negative Ofsted grade, the intake of a school tends to become more disadvantaged and teacher turnover increases, both of which contribute to the difficulty in reversing the negative Ofsted judgement.*

---

99   Teacher Tapp (2017) Is Ofsted 'Reliable & Trusted'? It Depends How You Ask... Blog post. *Teacher Tapp*. Available at: https://teachertapp.co.uk/articles/ofsted-reliable-trusted-depends-question-asl/

It states, 'we found evidence for a cycle of events in which poor Ofsted judgements play a modest contributory role in the onset of increasingly challenging circumstances, that then make it more likely that the school experiences further poor inspection grades in subsequent years.

'There was a vicious cycle between low Ofsted grades and increasingly deprived pupil intakes, and another between low Ofsted grades and increasing levels of teacher turnover. The effect sizes for these were small indicating that they are contributory factors but not the main determinants of schools becoming or remaining "stuck".'

The report's case studies highlight the reputational damage a poor Ofsted outcome can cause, which then leads to a snowball effect. The longer the school continues to have the less than good rating, the harder the process of school improvement becomes.

It adds: 'This reputational damage works as a slippery slope, as after receiving a below good grade, case study schools faced low staff and student morale, weak professional identity, difficult recruitment, lack of parental trust, among other challenges. "Un-stuck" schools described how this reputation was long-standing and very difficult to change, even after receiving a good grade.'[100]

Looking further into the original UCL report, we can see that not all its findings were negative:

Many 'stuck' and 'un-stuck' school stakeholders valued the role of Ofsted in general and inspectors in particular. Many described the key role of the inspectorate as providing accountability at the system level, to inform parents, and support schools to improve the quality of education through detailed diagnosis.

'Stuck' and 'un-stuck' schools valued the formal support received via LAs, MATs, Teaching Schools, advisories, etc. but also highlighted the key role of personal connections with inspectors, local schools, school improvement officers that trusted and supported them through time.

---

100 Henshaw, P. (2022) 'A vicious cycle' – poor Ofsted grades contribute to onset of challenging circumstances. *Headteacher Update*. 8 June. Available at: https://www. headteacher-update.com/news/a-vicious-cycle-poor-ofsted-grade-contributes-to-onset-of-challenging-circumstances-education-inspection-1/246376/

They valued opportunities for professional relatedness, people with whom they could share good practice without feeling intimidated.'

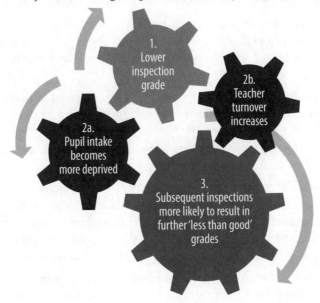

Figure 21. The vicious cycle[101]

However, another key finding was that some stakeholders raised concerns about the validity, reliability and fairness of inspections, including:

- Unfair comparisons and competition.
- Statistical driven judgements.
- Biased judgements.
- Unreliable inspection grades.
- Politicisation of inspection.
- Narrow focus on subjects which inform inspection judgements.
- Limitations in the progress measures.
- Pre-conceived inspector's judgements.
- Unacceptable behaviour from inspectors.

101 Munoz-Chereau, B., Hutchinson, J. and Ehren, M. (2022) *'Stuck' schools: Can below good Ofsted inspections prevent sustainable improvement?* London: UCL. Available at: https://epi.org.uk/wp-content/uploads/2022/06/Final_report_stuck_schools.pdf

- Bad inspection timing.

The report concludes with recommendations that Ofsted should:

- *Ensure that inspectors are properly trained to understand the significance and implications of schools working in very challenging circumstances, and the positive role they can play to support schools in their improvement journey.*

- *Consider what other positive support can be given to 'stuck' schools to assist in their improvement journey, including linking them with schools that have become 'un-stuck' or those that have specific expertise in areas that are core challenges, such as supporting children with EAL and/or refugee backgrounds.*

- *Revise the cycles of full section 5 inspections and monitoring section 8 inspections in order to give time to implement improvements. Avoid: a) transforming monitoring into too frequent inspections and over-surveillance; b) too much variation in the number of inspections and across inspectors; and c) providing false hope in monitoring inspections.*

- *Consider what changes in inspection can be implemented – for example removing overall grades – to avoid the detrimental effect that a series of below good Ofsted grades is having on school improvement, especially for schools working in challenging circumstances such as 'stuck' schools.*[102]

CAN WE TRUST OFSTED REPORTS?

An excellent question, and one which Ofsted sought to answer in their annual report for 2021-2022. In post-inspection surveys, they found that 92% of respondents felt satisfied with the way inspections were carried out and that 93% felt the inspection would help them improve their provision further (figure 22). Using the measure 'Do providers believe that their latest inspection was a fair and accurate assessment of the strengths and weaknesses of their provision?', figure 23 shows that the percentage of teachers who agree with this statement has actually increased over time from 57% in 2017 to 66% in 2022. It is no surprise that Ofsted defend themselves so robustly when this is what their own surveys tell them. There is so much conflicting evidence it can be hard for anyone to get a true picture, and this is one of the many reasons we need a large-scale review.

---

102 Ibid.

Responses to post-inspection surveys for inspections that took place between 1 April 2021 and 31 March 2022

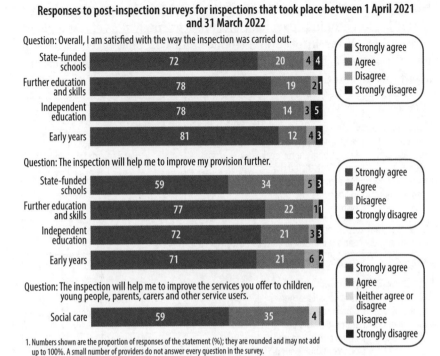

Figure 22. *Post-inspection survey responses*

Measure	Headline indicator	2017 baseline	2018	2019	2020	2021	2022
Providers believe that their latest inspection was a fair and accurate assessment of the strenths and weaknesses of their provision.	% of school teachers who agree that the following best describes their latest inspection: 'It was a fair and accurate assessment of the strengths and weaknesses of my school.'	57	62	61	No survey	No survey	66

Figure 23. *Do providers believe that their latest inspection was a fair and accurate assessment of the strengths and weaknesses of their provision?*[103]

103 Ofsted (2022) *Annual Report and Accounts 2021-22*. Available at: https://assets. publishing.service.gov.uk/government/uploads/system/uploads/attachment_data/ file/1090199/31252_Ofsted_Annual_Report_and_Accounts_2021-22__Print_.pdf

However, Ofsted also found that in 2019 only 20% of teachers agreed that Ofsted is a force for improvement, and, unsurprisingly, 84% of respondents agreed that 'Ofsted inspection introduced unacceptable levels of burden into the system' (figure 24). There are simply so many contradictions about Ofsted and the way its work is reported and portrayed.

Measure	Headline indicator*	2017 baseline	2018	2019	2020	2021	2022
We are increasingly seen as a force for improvement.	% of school teachers who strongly agree or agree that 'Ofsted is a force for improvement in England's education system.'	19	24	20	No data	No data	New indicator

*Data taken from responses to Ofsted's post-inspection survey. Data available here: https://www.gov.uk/government/collections/responses-to-ofsteds-post-inspection-surveys.

Measure	Headline indicator*	2017 baseline	2018	2019	2020	2021	2022
We reduce the unintended consequences of inspection.	% of school teachers who agree with the statement: 'Ofsted inspection introduced unacceptable levels of burden into the system.'	86	82	84	No data	No data	No data

Figure 24. A force for improvement and unintended consequences.

In 2012, the DfE made 'outstanding' primary and secondary schools exempt from routine inspection. Ofsted remind us that they, 'could still inspect exempt schools if we had concerns. These concerns could be triggered by a risk assessment (based on data such as school performance data, workforce data, contextual data and complaints); or by a significant change to the school (such as taking on an extra key stage).' The movement of schools into and out of the 'outstanding' zone during the period of exemption is shown in figure 25.[104]

104 Ofsted (2022) *A return to inspection: the story (so far) of previously exempt outstanding schools*. Available at: https://www.gov.uk/government/publications/school-inspections-statistical-commentaries-2021-to-2022/a-return-to-inspection-the-story-so-far-of-previously-exempt-outstanding-schools

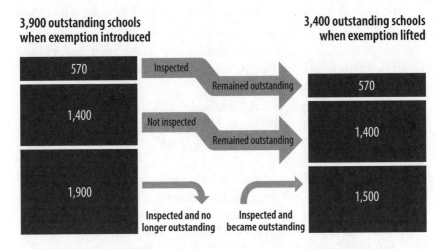

Figure 25. Changes in the cohort of outstanding exempt schools, 2012 to 2020

As we saw earlier, in the year following the end of the exemption, with around 370 schools inspected in 2021-2022, 17% remained 'outstanding', 62% became 'good' and 21% were judged 'requires improvement' or 'inadequate' (figure 26).

Figure 26. Outcomes of graded inspections of previously exempt schools in 2021/22 by phase

It was not just across stages that variances could be seen:

- Selective schools such as grammar schools were more likely to remain 'outstanding' than non-selective schools, and less likely to be judged 'requires improvement' or 'inadequate' even when they received a lower grade.

- In 2021/22, the academies were more likely than maintained schools to remain 'outstanding'. This was the case for both primary and secondary schools.

- There was a mixed picture for schools of different faiths, but overall faith schools were slightly more likely to remain 'outstanding' than non-faith schools. The vast majority of faith schools inspected were Christian schools.

- 30% of secondary schools in the areas of most deprivation were judged to be 'requires improvement' versus 20% 'requires improvement' and 'inadequate' in the least deprived areas. Although interestingly, none of the secondary schools in the most deprived areas were judged 'inadequate', whereas 12% were in the areas of least deprivation.

Figure 27. Outcomes of graded inspection of previously exempt schools in 2021/22 by deprivation.[105]

105 Ofsted (2022) *A return to inspection: the story (so far) of previously exempt outstanding schools.* Available at: https://www.gov.uk/government/publications/school-inspections-statistical-commentaries-2021-to-2022/a-return-to-inspection-the-story-so-far-of-previously-exempt-outstanding-schools

OFSTED COMPLAINTS

A Government paper written in 2021 explains that, 'providers who are unhappy about the way an inspection is being carried out are encouraged to discuss any concerns with the inspection team. There should also be an opportunity for the school to fact-check a draft of the resulting report for accuracy.' It adds that if providers are still unhappy with the outcome of an Ofsted inspection there are additional steps that can be taken. The paper emphasises that after following internal complaints procedures, schools and other providers may also be able to complain to the Independent Complaints Adjudication Service for Ofsted (ICASO) who can consider complaints about a range of issues including alleged discourtesy during inspections, failure to apologise or accept mistakes, and failure to follow procedures, but it cannot overturn inspectors' judgements. This last point is the most contentious. Individuals or private organisations unsatisfied with the outcome of an ICASO review may be able to ask the Parliamentary and Health Service Ombudsman to look at the issue.[106] When we look into this issue, we can see that the percentage of complaints as a proportion of the number of inspections is small (figure 28).

Period	Inspection/ activites*	Complaints received**	Proportion of total	Proportion of closed complaints responded to within 30 days***
2021-22	30,609	635	2.07%	97%
2020-21	20,096	67	0.30%	90%
2019-20	35,763	890	2.50%	93%

Fig 28. Percentage of complaints received by Ofsted as a proportion of all inspections carried out.[107]

---

106 Roberts, N. and Hill, R. (2021) *School inspections in England: Ofsted*. London: House of Commons Library.

107 Ofsted (2022) *Annual Report and Accounts 2021-22*. Available at: https://assets. publishing.service.gov.uk/government/uploads/system/uploads/attachment_ data/file/1090199/31252_Ofsted_Annual_Report_and_Accounts_2021-22__ Print_.pdf

IS OFSTED FIT FOR PURPOSE?

The educational equivalent of being in the stocks is being put in an Ofsted category.

Carl Smith, Principal

Is it fit for purpose? Well, it depends on who you ask and what their view of 'purpose' is. Personal experience is a huge factor here. As we have read, experiences of inspections vary, positively and negatively, and we can't argue with how people feel or how the process made them feel at the time. We have seen issues around the changing frameworks, misinterpretation by some, and the differences in tone set by the lead inspector themselves. We have read that the purpose of inspection is to hold schools to account with a view to improving all schools.

How far is Ofsted driven by politics and politicians themselves? The correlation between the purpose of Ofsted and the current political leadership and their view of education is an important one. Over time party politics change and so do views on what a great education system should look like, which will affect how it is measured. I've heard someone recently say that Ofsted are in a moral panic about safeguarding. No one would disagree that safeguarding has to be effective. However, somehow it has gone too far, with the school being responsible for the safety of the child not only in school, but also out of school, and even being made to feel responsible for things like online safety at home.

WHAT ABOUT OFSTED RESEARCH?

Ofsted is currently striving to be a research-led organisation. Is this helpful? Or is it a distraction, and a diversion of funds that could be spent on schools? Even in 2021, Ofsted published plenty of research reports, as shown below.[108]

---

108 Ofsted (2022) *Annual Report and Accounts 2021-22*. London: HMSO. Available at: https://assets.publishing.service.gov.uk/government/uploads/system/uploads/attachment_data/file/1090199/31252_Ofsted_Annual_Report_and_Accounts_2021-22__Print_.pdf

- 'Review of sexual abuse in schools and colleges': this rapid thematic review revealed how prevalent sexual harassment and online sexual abuse are for children and young people. It made recommendations for schools and college leaders, multi-agency partners and government.

- A series of reports on education recovery in schools, further education and skills, and early years providers: these briefings drew on evidence from inspections during autumn 2021 and spring 2022 that reported on the continued impact of the pandemic and education recovery.

- 'Securing good attendance and tackling persistent absence': this short report looked at different aspects of attendance and how schools tackle the challenges they face.

- 'Supporting SEND': this report considered how the needs of children and young people with SEND are met in mainstream schools and how approaches vary between providers.

- 'SEND: old issues, new issues, next steps': this research summarised the experiences of children and young people with SEND and their families during the pandemic, in the context of the SEND reforms over the past 10 years.

- 'Teaching teachers during COVID-19': this evaluative report looked at how the ITE sector has responded to COVID-19 and how the ITE curriculum has been developed.

- Subject research reviews, including on science, religious education, mathematics, languages, geography, music, history and PE.

- 'Prison education: a review of reading education in prisons': this study highlighted the systemic barriers that prevent prisoners from receiving effective support to acquire or improve their reading skills. We also published a commentary on what has been happening to adult education in prisons during the pandemic.

- 'How groups of children's homes work': this report explored how groups of children's homes operate.

- 'How early years multiple providers work': this report explored the roles and responsibilities within early years multiple providers in determining the quality and standards of early years provision. It focused on understanding how multiple providers influence policy and practice across individual nurseries and pre-schools.

- '"Ready or not": care leavers' views of preparing to leave care': this research looked at the planning and preparation that happen before a young person leaves care.

- 'Early help: concepts, policy directions and multi-agency perspectives': this scoping study, commissioned by Ofsted and carried out by Research in Practice, looked at how responsive early help and local multi-agency partnerships are in meeting the needs of children, young people and their families.

What if one role of a reformed inspectorate was to inspect schools around the country, having abandoned the grading activity and actually look nationally at what works and what doesn't? At the moment there is confusion about Ofsted's research and report writing activity and its role as an inspectorate. Is Ofsted here to measure and judge with a straightforward accountability approach, or is it here to support and challenge? In the latter scenario, their own research is much welcomed. Support by offering best practice and then challenge to see if this is implemented and with what results sounds great. It is, however, hard to see them as doing both in the current environment. In some cases, the Ofsted subject papers are narrow in their scope and have led to real prescription in what inspectors want to see, and are in fact told to look for. The current preoccupation with memory is a case in point. Some schools are using much more learning time for memorising than necessary just to show inspectors that pupils 'know more'. Hearing inspectors sigh when children can't remember in December what they learned in September is testament to this. Using professionals and expert practitioners in a broader self-improving system would be welcomed by many, and the narrow research focus of Ofsted could be supported by other organisations such as the Education Endowment Fund (EEF).

Helena McVeigh writes that currently 'the purpose of inspection is to identify, for a school and its parents, what is going well and what needs to improve. It is not designed to stand up to the scrutiny of published research, which would take far too long to be useful to schools and its parents'.[109] I think we would agree that Ofsted attempting to use its own inspection findings as research is not 'real evidence'. The papers listed above might be better received if Ofsted were trusted more, and that trust could be created by opening their own research up to peer review.

109 McVeigh, H. (2020) *Teaching and the role of Ofsted.* London: UCL-IOE press.

CHAPTER 7
COMPARATIVE ACCOUNTABILITY SYSTEMS

Nearly all countries have a school inspectorate of some kind. In some countries the inspection model seems more punitive, and in others less so.

Writing for the National Education Union, Jane Perryman highlights some of the options:

> *It is possible to have a more supportive inspectorate – for example in some countries, among them Austria, Iceland, and Denmark, inspections do not place sanctions on low-performing schools and do not make reports public, which takes the pressure off schools to perform, so they can get support with issues requiring attention. Functions of inspection can be categorised along a continuum of support and control, and different inspection regimes have different purposes according to which function they prioritise. Some countries adopt a low stakes capacity building approach, others operate at a level of powerful high stakes enforcement. There seems little doubt that Ofsted is in the latter category, and is, it seems, incapable of fundamental change, even in extraordinary circumstances. Only an alternative system can provide the support that our schools deserve.[110]*

Let's start by staying local and looking at the other three nations in the United Kingdom. I have begun to put together a comparison of school inspection features across the UK (figure 29).

---

110 Perryman, J. (2022) Ofsted is more stick than carrot. Blog post. *NEU*. Available at: https://neu.org.uk/blog/ofsted-more-stick-carrot

Country	School inspection body	Announced inspection times	Inspection cycles	Judgements are made about…	Main outcomes of inspection
England	Ofsted / Independent School Inspectorate	24 hours	4 years	• The quality of education. • Behaviour and attitudes. • Personal development. • Leadership and management. • Sixth form and EYFS if appropriate.	Overall judgement of effectiveness. Grade 1 – outstanding. Grade 2 – good. Grade 3 – requires improvement. Grade 4 – inadequate. A report which outlines what the school does well and what it needs to do to improve further.
Northern Ireland	The Education and Training Inspectorate (Northern Ireland) (ETI)	Currently under consultation and review.			
Wales	Estyn is the inspectorate for state-funded schools, independent schools and many other type of provider in Wales.	10 days	8 years	• Inspection area 1 – Outcomes. • Inspection area 2 – Education Services. • Inspection area 3 – Leadership and management.	Inspectors will evaluate and report on all aspects of inspection areas 1 and 3 of the framework. Inspection area 2 of the framework sets out the scope of services that could be inspected during an inspection.

| Scotland | Education Scotland | Two and a half weeks. | Schools are inspected on a proportionate basis, using a sampling approach, rather than a cyclical model. | Five main Quality Indicators are used in full inspections of Primary and Secondary. 4 are mandatory (1.3 Leadership of change. 2.3 Learning, teaching and assessment. 3.2 Raising attainment and achievement. 3.1 Ensuring wellbeing, equality and inclusion.) The final QI is chosen by the school. | As part of each inspection process, they will form a set of local inspection questions about education services. Inspectors will evaluate services covered by these questions and report on each question separately within the report. | Summarised Inspection Findings (SIF). The inspection team will publish a letter for parents on the Education Scotland website. |

Figure 29. School inspection in England, Wales, Scotland and Northern Ireland

NORTHERN IRELAND

The current handbook used in inspections in Northern Ireland was created collaboratively, with schools and practitioners working with the ETI to write the indicators used in the booklet *Together Towards Improvement* which is, 'promoted for use in self-evaluation for improvement and made available to schools'.[111]

However, I have deliberately left the Northern Ireland section blank in the table because inspections have been boycotted there since 2016 (except for a few follow-up and intervention visits). To find out what was happening I spoke to a senior teacher union official in Northern Ireland. They said there had been industrial action about both pay and workload conditions since this time and that as inspection added a great deal of workload they came under this action.

The inspection model had been that inspections were conducted every seven years for schools judged to be 'good' and a review every three years for schools judged 'excellent'. I was told that in some cases schools didn't want the 'excellent' judgement because of the increased frequency of review it entails and were happier to be labelled as 'good'. School leaders felt that inspection teams were not taking context into account, a criticism also levelled at English inspection teams. Interestingly I learned that the Chief Inspector from 2011 to 2020 was previously at Ofsted, and that the new Chief Inspector, in post since 2020, was heralding a new approach to school inspection. Apparently, the new framework will be a more collaborative venture, co-designed between different stakeholders including teachers and the unions. This new approach should empower people in the system who will have their views heard. Pilot inspections will occur, as in England, and evaluations of these will also include voices from others such as the students themselves. It was unclear whether grades will be removed but this is under discussion. The unions are also looking at the complaints procedures with a view to employing a more independent body to implement them. The official I spoke with said this 'is a real opportunity to create an inspection model which is the envy of others'. We talked about the role of District Inspectors who oversee 20 to 40 schools

---

111 Gray, A. (2019) *European School Inspection and Evaluation.* Nottingham: Bookworm of Retford

who could rebuild the relationship between the Inspectorate and schools and support school improvement as a partner. Inspections would focus on identifying strengths and areas to work on, but with advice on 'here's how'. This consultation work is in process as I write and I look forward to seeing what comes next in Northern Ireland.

WALES

In a change from the previous process of inspection, Wales have removed the grades from their school inspection reports. Estyn have said that their reports will focus instead on 'how well providers are helping a child to learn'. The inspection teams will produce:

- A key overview of findings to be included in the report headline focusing on a school's strengths and areas for development.

- A separate report summary for parents which will allow parents to access the key information they need about an inspection quickly.

Estyn say their new inspections will have a different approach, and come into force at the same time as the introduction of a new curriculum, one less fixated on knowledge retention and more on four key purposes of education. They envisage the new process to be more personalised, involving more discussions, and they 'believe our new inspection approach will make it easier for providers to gain meaningful insights that help them to improve without the spotlight on a judgement'. Estyn has retained the statutory categories of special measures and significant improvement.[112]

Estyn list five key principles of inspection (figure 30) which are worth taking the time to reflect on in light of what we have read about the current system in England.

---

112 Estyn (2022) *Inspection Explained*. Available at: https://www.estyn.gov.wales/inspection-process/inspection-explained

Figure 30. Estyn principles of inspection[113] © Crown Copyright

113 Estyn (nd) *The Principles of Inspection.* Available at: https://www.estyn.gov.wales/sites/
www.estyn.gov.wales/files/2021-08/Inspection%20principles%20infographic.pdf

Estyn has also published guidance for their inspectors. The section on inspecting the school self-evaluation processes and improvement planning is particularly interesting and much more detailed than the current Ofsted framework. It outlines that, 'Inspectors should evaluate how accurately leaders and managers know the school's strengths and weaknesses. They should focus on the effectiveness and impact of the school's self-evaluation and improvement processes, rather than the quality of documentation.' One of the criticisms of the imposed self-evaluation form we used to have to produce for Ofsted was that it was often lengthy and at worst written by external consultants. However, I do believe we should return to some sort of form, maybe one with a word count that had to be signed off by a school improvement partner (SIP), as I do believe it helps inspectors learn how we see ourselves. It is the 'effectiveness and impact of the school's self-evaluation and improvement processes, rather than the quality of documentation' which is most appealing. It directs that the report should contain a short overview of the main findings (400-500 words), outlining the key strengths and any important weaknesses that require improvement. No grades, just what the school does well, which it encourages schools to write up as case studies, and recommendations which should:

- link closely to the main evaluation areas of the inspection guidance, with the weightiest recommendations reflected in the overview
- give the provider a clear and specific indication of the area(s) that require improvement
- help the provider to understand clearly what they should do to make the necessary improvements.

Estyn say their inspectors should consider how well the school or PRU:

1. involves all of its staff, as well as a wide range of partners, including pupils and parents
2. gathers and analyses robust first-hand evidence of standards and provision
3. maintains a clear focus on the impact of its provision on pupil progress and wellbeing
4. uses self-evaluation findings, together with other information, to devise relevant priorities and actions for improvement

5. sets specific, realistic timescales and allocates appropriate responsibility for securing improvement

6. supports improvement priorities through the appropriate allocation of resources

7. ensures that spending decisions and financial planning link appropriately to its strategic improvement priorities including effective use of the PDG

8. monitors and evaluates progress against its priorities and adapts its approaches where necessary

9. uses evaluative approaches to assure leaders and governors of the effective operation of key policies and procedures, for example in relation to safeguarding.

Points 1 – 3 are not much different to what any inspection team would do, but points 5 – 9 demonstrate much more of what looks like a collaborative approach. A 'done with', not 'done to' model of inspection. Estyn also hopes to be pragmatic in that they will pay regard to the fact that the Welsh Curriculum itself is also new and schools will only have started to implement it in September 2022. They say, 'during the period of familiarisation and implementation of the Curriculum for Wales, we will adopt a pragmatic approach to the provider's work to plan, design and realise their curriculum in an appropriate and timely manner.' In England, much criticism has been levelled at Ofsted for not showing such pragmatism when imposing the current framework on schools, particularly given that we have just emerged from a global pandemic, and that in many cases little or no consideration of this has been taken into account.[114]

Estyn also use the word 'context' here – which is currently missing from the Ofsted approach or understanding – adding, 'inspectors will approach their evaluation of the school or PRUs curriculum taking account of the provider's vision, context and rationale for developing their bespoke curriculum in line with the requirements for Curriculum for Wales.' With regards to attendance, 'when considering well-being and attitudes to learning, inspectors will not report on the school's attendance rate

---

114 Estyn (2022) *Guidance for Inspectors. What we Inspect.* Available at: https://www.estyn.gov.wales/system/files/2022-09/What%20we%20inspect%20-%202022_0.pdf

compared with other similar schools. However, we will consider the effectiveness of the school's approaches to ensure that pupils attend school and engage with their learning on a regular basis, as part of their evaluation of the school's provision for care, support and guidance.' It would seem that pragmatism, and maybe even compassion informs their approach!

Estyn shares the proposed mindset and approach of the inspection team:

- *Fair and impartial – this means that we work to be independent, objective and balanced. We are robust and consistent in our work. We weigh the evidence and its significance to provide an honest, credible and accurate view of the provider's strengths and areas for improvement.*

- *Supportive – we work to guide providers to implement improvements that benefit learners. We encourage innovation and recognise good intentions. We are friendly but always professional in our approach. We support educational reform. We work hard to develop meaningful relationships with providers and local and regional organisations.*

- *Reflective – we are open-minded. We listen to a wide range of stakeholders and reflect on their responses. We are thoughtful, measured and careful. We plan opportunities to think carefully about the inspection findings and to discuss them with others in the team.*

- *Transparent – we are well informed and communicate clearly, directly and succinctly. We use efficient and effective inspection methodologies to respond to the provider's unique situation. We plan inspection activity and report on strengths and weaknesses in ways that reflect the particular circumstances of each individual provider. As a result, our actions promote trust and respect.*

The inspection team itself is made up of members with different roles. The team will include a Reporting Inspector (RI), also known as the lead inspector. They will be either a HMI civil servant, an additional Inspector (AI) who will be seconded from schools or other providers, or a Registered Inspector (RgI), who are trained and qualified lead inspectors contracted to lead specific inspections. Not much difference here so far. What is different is that these teams will also include a Peer Inspector

(PI) who is another serving inspector from another school or PRU, and a Lay Inspector (LI) who is not a qualified teacher but who might have some experience in community work of some kind, brought in to bring a different non-specialist dimension to the team's work. In addition, providers are invited to select a senior member of their own staff body to work with the inspection team. It will be very interesting to see how well these teams work together and to ascertain what gains have been made by expanding the membership of the teams.[115]

SCOTLAND

The inspection model in Scotland works with schools to make judgements around a set of 15 Quality Indicators (QIs). These QIs, 'are designed to enable providers to undertake self-evaluation leading to improvement. The QIs also form the framework used by HM Inspectors to evaluate the quality of education provision as part of inspection and review.' Inspection teams use these QIs to, 'identify and report what is working well; what needs to improve and examples of highly effective and sector leading practice. We let providers know which QIs or themes within QIs we will be evaluating in advance.'[116]

From these, inspectors will report on a section according to the type of provider (see figure 31), for example, in schools five main QIs are used in full inspections:

- 1.3 Leadership of change.
- 2.3 Learning, teaching and assessment.
- 3.2 Raising attainment and achievement.
- 3.1 Ensuring wellbeing, equality and inclusion.
- The final QI is chosen by the school. (This is not graded within the HGIOS six-point scale).

---

115 Estyn (2022) *Guidance for Inspectors. How we Inspect.* Available at: https://www.estyn.gov.wales/system/files/2022-10/How%20we%20inspect%202022.pdf

116 Education Scotland (nd) *Evaluating quality and improvement in Scottish education.* Available at: https://education.gov.scot/education-scotland/what-we-do/inspection-and-review/standards-and-evaluation-framework/01-evaluating-quality-and-improvement-in-scottish-education/

These areas have commonalities with Ofsted headings though the inspectors are more concerned with school improvement activities and managing change, with no single overall grade.

For inspection of nursery classes, four main QIs are used:

- 1.3 Leadership of change.
- 2.3 Learning, teaching and assessment.
- 3.2 Securing children's progress.
- 3.1 Ensuring wellbeing, equality and inclusion.

Each of these indicators is awarded a grade:

- Excellent
- Very good
- Good
- Satisfactory
- Weak
- Unsatisfactory

'Education Scotland believes that the inspection process is about how effectively the school/education setting uses self-evaluation to take forward its plan to improve.' Their ambition is that, 'Our inspections provide the opportunity for early learning and childcare settings and schools to show that they know themselves inside out and that they are using self-evaluation to focus on improving all the achievements of children.'[117] Though we have moved away from these as a common document in England, headteachers in Scotland are asked to complete a SEF in advance of inspection. Headteachers will use this SEF at the start of the inspection, to brief the inspection team on the impact of the school's approach to improvement through self-evaluation.

---

117 Educational Institute of Scotland (2019) *Education Scotland Inspections. General. Advice for Members.* Available at: https://www.eis.org.uk/Content/images/Policies/ AGM%202018%202%20EIS%20Inspection%20Advice%20-%20General.pdf

What is our capacity for improvement?		
Leadership and management	**Learning provision**	**Successes and achievements**
How good is our leadership and approach to improvement?	How good is the quality of the care and education we offer?	How good are we at ensuring the best possible outcomes for all our learners?
1.1 Self-evaluation for self-improvement	**2.1** Safeguarding and child protection	**3.1** Ensuring wellbeing, equality and inclusion
1.2 Leadership for learning	**2.2** Curriculum	**3.2** Raising attainment and achievement
1.3 Leadership for change	**2.3** Learning, teaching and assessment	**3.3** Increasing creativity and employability
1.4 Leadership and management of staff	**2.4** Personalised support	
1.5 Management of resources to promote equity	**2.5** Family learning	
	2.6 Transitions	
	2.7 Partnerships	

Figure 31. Quality Indicators used in inspections in Scotland

On receipt of the notification email, headteachers are also advised of the evidence that is required to be completed in advance of the inspection (school self-evaluation, the safeguarding proforma and online stakeholder questionnaires) and of the other existing school documentation to be shared with the inspection team, such as the current and recent school improvement plans. What is also different here is the expectation to submit a record of safeguarding.

As with Estyn, there may be additional members in the inspecting team. There may be additional permanent HM Inspectors of Education, a health and nutrition inspector (HNI), assistant inspectors or associate assessors. The team will also include a Care Inspector where nursery settings/ classes are being inspected. Inspection teams may also include lay members who are members of the public, trained by Education Scotland staff, who have an interest in, but no professional involvement with, education.[118]

These inspection regimes raise a number of interesting points for us to consider. As in Northern Ireland, we should stop and take stock about the purpose of school inspection and how it should happen. We should look at Estyn and consider removing the grades, and at both the Welsh and Scottish practice of widening the experience of inspectors to make inspections more relevant and more appreciative of context.

SCHOOL ACCOUNTABILITY ELSEWHERE

The NFER produced some thumbnail sketches of accountability in schools in four other countries, which I have summarised here.

In Australia (New South Wales), there is statutory national assessment in the primary phase. The assessments are used to hold schools to account. School evaluation involves a process of statutory annual self-assessment. In a five-year cycle, school self-assessments are validated by an external panel. There is a mechanism of peer-to-peer support for school improvement.

Japan operates a system of statutory external evaluation which does include school inspection. In Japan, there is a statutory requirement for school self-evaluation and there is a mechanism for school-to-school support for school improvement.

In New Zealand national monitoring does not produce information about individual students, teachers or schools. There is statutory evaluation of schools in New Zealand, and this does include inspection. School self-evaluation is a statutory requirement.

Singapore operates a self-assessment model (the School Excellence Model, or SEM). Within this framework, schools self-evaluate and also undergo external validation.

---

118 Ibid.

We can see common threads of self-evaluation, externally validated in Australia, and with peer-to-peer support in Australia and Japan, both of which I see as crucial parts of a reform to our current inspection model here in England.[119]

WHAT HAPPENS IN THE PRIVATE SECTOR AND THE INDEPENDENT SCHOOL INSPECTORATE (ISI)?

The ISI reports directly to the DfE on how far independent schools meet their standards. These Independent School Standards (set by the DfE) are shown in figure 32. ISI reports make judgements about a school's compliance with these standards and any action it must take to meet them. Recommendations may also be made to help schools identify and address any areas for improvement and build on good practice.

The inspections can be either routine or non-routine:

Routine inspections are announced, and schools get a two-day notice period. A school can expect one of each type every three years. They include:

- Regulatory Compliance Inspection (RCI): This inspection checks that a school's policies and practices are compliant with the regulations set by the Department for Education.
- Educational Quality with Focused Compliance (EQI): This inspection looks at the quality of education a school provides and checks a targeted section of policies and practices. The EQI reports on the two main outcomes for pupils; achievement and personal development.

Non-routine inspections include:

- Progress monitoring: This occurs when a school has failed to meet the standards on a scheduled inspection and is visited for a second time to inspect for improvement.

---

119 Brill, F., Grayson, H., Kuhn, L. and O'Donnell, S. (2018) *What Impact Does Accountability Have On Curriculum, Standards and Engagement In Education? A Literature Review*. Slough: NFER. Available at: https://www.nfer.ac.uk/media/3032/nfer_accountability_literature_review_2018.pdf

- Additional: This occurs when the Department for Education has reason for a school to be inspected urgently.

Independent School Standards

- Quality of leadership in and management of schools

- Quality of education

- Spiritual, Moral, Social and Cultural development of pupils

- Welfare, health and safety of pupils

- Suitability of staff, supply staff and proprietors

- Premises of and accommodation at schools

- Provision of information

- Manner in which complaints are handled

Figure 32. The Independent School Standards[120]

The ISI does not make a single overarching judgement on a school. Instead, they make a clear judgement on each aspect of its work using one of the following four grades: excellent, good, sound or unsatisfactory, although I have heard that the use of these grades is currently under review.[121]

---

120 ISI (nd) *The Independent School Standards*. Available at: https://www.isi.net/inspections/the-independent-school-standards
121 The full ISI inspection framework can be found at: https://www.isi.net/site/downloads/1.1%20Handbook%20Inspection%20Framework%202019-09.pdf

STATUTORY INSPECTION OF ANGLICAN AND METHODIST SCHOOLS (SIAMS)

Apart from any one school having to be 'inspected twice' what does this approach look like? Both judgements are valuable to schools and their communities, and both are worth fighting for.

> *The evaluation schedule has one inspection question: 'How effective is the school's distinctive Christian vision, established and promoted by leadership at all levels, in enabling pupils and adults to flourish?' This is explored through seven strands:*
>
> *1. Vision and Leadership*
>
> *2. Wisdom, Knowledge, and Skills*
>
> *3. Character Development: Hope, Aspiration, and Courageous Advocacy*
>
> *4. Community and Living Well Together*
>
> *5. Dignity and Respect*
>
> *6. Impact of Collective Worship*
>
> *7. Effectiveness of Religious Education.*
>
> *As it stands one overall grade is awarded reflecting the contribution of these strands to the flourishing of pupils and adults in a Church school.*[122]

However, from September 2023, there will be no grades awarded. Writing for *Schools Week* in 2023, Margaret James, the national director of SIAMS, says that, 'instead, an inspector will make a judgement on whether the school is living up to its Anglican/Methodist foundation through an up-to-date Christian vision that enables all pupils and adults to flourish ... it will provide a narrative account of the school's strengths and areas for development.' The article notes that, 'inspection criteria have been dispensed with, respectfully allowing school leaders the freedom to apply their expertise in serving the needs of their

---

122 The Church Of England (nd) *SIAMS Inspections.* Available at: https://www.churchofengland.org/about/education-and-schools/church-schools-and-academies/siams-inspections

communities. The school will be asked to provide evidence of the impact of their work and the inspector will use the evidence to make a judgement on whether the school is living up to its foundation as a Church school.' It is interesting to read that there will be no generic criteria against which to make judgements but that the new framework, 'invites leaders to demonstrate how the vision is being worked out in practice and in context.' The outcome of an inspection will be, 'one of two evidence based judgements: The school will either be deemed to be living up to its foundation as a Church school, or inspectors will set out the reasons why it may not be fully doing so.' This new approach is hoped to be more collaborative, one that takes school context into account and one that recognises 'the professionalism and expertise of school leaders and focusing exclusively on the impact of actions rather than on the actions themselves'. Sounds very attractive![123]

A LOOK AT TWO OTHER PUBLIC SERVICES

There are several other public services in England that are also held to account through inspectorates; although they are different in their operations and scope it may be interesting to try and make some brief comparisons. Is grading involved, is there self-evaluation, are outcomes published, are stakeholders involved? What follows is a tiny snapshot of inspection features in a range of public services. It is only a small investigation for the purposes of comparison and I apologise if any nuance or fine detail has been omitted.

THE POLICE FORCE

The Police Force in England, Wales and Northern Ireland is held to account by HM Inspectorate of Constabulary and Fire & Rescue Services (HMICFRS) who independently assess and report on the efficiency and effectiveness of police forces and policing, in the public interest.

---

123 James, M. (2023) Why we've ditched the grades from SIAMS inspections. *Schools Week*. 18 March. Available at: https://schoolsweek.co.uk/why-weve-ditched-the-grades-from-siams-inspections/#:~:text=For%20almost%20three%20decades%2C%20they,no%20longer%20be%20the%20case

The objectives of inspections are to:

- improve the services they provide and to ensure they reduce the risks identified by local communities
- identify good practice, transformation and areas for improvement
- improve transparency and accountability to the communities they serve.

HMICFRS inspects and monitors the 43 territorial police forces in England and Wales. It publishes an inspection programme annually, including a schedule of inspections. This schedule includes the inspections called the PEEL assessments. PEEL stands for police effectiveness, efficiency and legitimacy. There are 43 Home Office-funded police forces, each assigned to one of four geographic regions, with each region being overseen by one of His Majesty's Inspectors of Constabulary.[124]

Their approach is 'an intelligence-led continuous assessment model', which gathers a variety of evidence from a range of sources including:

- the relevant police and crime plan
- the relevant force management statement
- findings from thematic and joint inspections
- crime data integrity inspections
- progress against established causes of concern and areas for improvement
- routine data collections
- knowledge gained through regular liaison between the force and the inspectorate
- evidence collected through regular engagement with the force, in order to gain insight into its activities.

On-site inspections as well as information gathered from the above help the inspectorate arrive at judgements for each force. Each force completes a self-assessment form annually and HMICFRS use these to inform their inspections of forces' efficiency, effectiveness and legitimacy, to inform

---

124 HMICFRS (nd) *Who we inspect*. Available at: https://www.justiceinspectorates.gov.uk/hmicfrs/about-us/who-we-inspect/

their thematic inspections, and to supplement their monitoring of forces' performance.

This self-assessment form has several sections that need to be filled in by each force and includes:

Part 1:

Summary including a strategic risk assessment summary.

Part 2:

Section 1: Finance.

Section 2: Wellbeing.

Section 3a: Responding to the public – requests for service.

Section 3b: Responding to the public – incident response.

Section 4: Prevention and deterrence (neighbourhood policing).

Section 5: Investigations.

Section 6: Protecting vulnerable people.

Section 7: Managing offenders.

Section 8: Managing serious and organised crime.

Section 9: Major events.

Section 10: Knowledge management and information & communications. technology (ICT)

Section 11: Force-wide functions.

Section 12: Collaboration.

In most of the sections listed, the self-assessment form requires narrative around the following four steps:

Step 1: Establish the gap between current demand and demand you expect in the foreseeable future or the next four years.

Step 2: Establish the current and future status of your workforce and other assets: their performance, condition, capacity, capability, serviceability, wellbeing and security of supply.

Step 3: Explain what you will do to make sure that your workforce and other assets can meet the demand you are anticipating. Describe the expected effects of the planned changes and how these will be monitored.

Step 4: Estimate the extent of future demand that you expect to be met having made the changes and efficiencies in Step 3. You should state any demand that you expect to be unmet and what the consequences of not meeting it are expected to be.

As with Ofsted inspections these areas are then graded:

Outstanding – The force has substantially exceeded the characteristics of good performance.

Good – The force has demonstrated substantially all the characteristics of good performance.

Adequate – The force has demonstrated some of the characteristics of good performance, but we have identified areas where the force should make improvements.

Requires improvement – The force has demonstrated few, if any, of the characteristics of good performance and we have identified a substantial number of areas where the force needs to make improvements.

Inadequate – We have causes for concern and have made recommendations to the force to address them.

Unlike Ofsted reports the PEEL assessments award these grades in separate categories so that any force could be seen to have strengths in a particular area with no overall judgement. This then leads to continued support and monitoring for the areas that are weaker, not as we have in school inspections, where if the overall grade is good then the school is 'left alone'. Also, unlike Ofsted, the inspections and judgements pay great attention to the 'local policing body's police and crime plan for the force, in order to be clear on its established local priorities' and there is a clear expectation that each force's FMS must be, 'sensitive to, and reflective of, local conditions and circumstances.' This appreciation of local context is another significant difference.

The different areas to be judged are set out below, with each force given a separate grade against each of these, but not an overall grade.

It would be interesting to see if parents would appreciate the individual breakdown of grades given by Ofsted more than the overall grade, and if using reports in this way would be of greater assistance to their decision making.

Providing a service to the victims of crime
Recording data about crime
Engaging with and treating the public with fairness and respect
Preventing crime and anti-social behaviour
Responding to the public
Investigating crime
Protecting vulnerable people
Managing offenders and suspects
Disrupting serious organised crime
Building, supporting and protecting the workforce
Tackling workforce corruption
Strategic planning, organisational management and value for money[125]

THE HEALTH SERVICE

The Health Service is another body that is inspected and where grades are awarded, but again grades are given for individual areas.

---

125 HMICFRS (nd) *PEEL assessments 2021/22*. Available at: https://www.justiceinspectorates.gov.uk/hmicfrs/peel-assessments/peel-assessments-2021-22/

As a regulatory body, the Care Quality Commission collects evidence to judge standards across six categories including:

- people's experiences
- feedback for staff and leaders
- observations of care
- feedback from partners
- processes
- outcomes of care.

They ask five key questions which all go into 'quality statements' to see if provisions are safe, effective, caring, responsive and well-led.

So, for example, to be effective a provider should be able to assess needs, deliver evidence-based care and treatment, show that staff, teams and services work well together, that they support people to live healthier lives, and that they monitor and improve outcomes. When you search for a hospital each of these is given a grade.

Safe	Good ●
Effective	Good ●
Caring	Outstanding ☆
Responsive	Good ●
Well-led	Good ●

In addition, grades are awarded for each specific service including medical care, services for children and young people, critical care and other specialisms a hospital might have:

Medical care (including older people's care)	30 August 2018	Good	●
Services for children & young people	14 July 2016	Good	●
Critical care	14 July 2016	Good	●
Hospital Dental Services			
End of life care	14 July 2016	Good	●
Maternity	14 December 2022	Good	●
Outpatients	30 August 2018	Good	●
Surgery	14 July 2016	Good	●
Urgent and emergency services	30 August 2018	Good	●

For the user this is very helpful as one might be interested in a specific aspect and be reassured that for that aspect the hospital performs well.

This approach is not dissimilar to school inspection frameworks: there are four ratings and a scoring framework to show how the view of quality was formed. In fact, I believe the CQC grading approach was adapted from that of Ofsted during a meeting of ministers. To help me understand the similarities and differences in accountability between these two sectors I spoke with someone who worked for CQC and helped develop some of the inspection processes. I have used some of their comments and thoughts to help form a reflection on inspections in schools.

The question in this public sector about regulation and inspection approaches is the same. Does it lead to improvement? There is no research that proves this and many accounts that say it absolutely does not. If regulation says you have failed, then it's too late and if it says you are a good provider then you probably know this already. When we reflect on this, we can see that we might need a continuous improvement and review methodology to ensure schools improve, not a two-day blunt instrument, the outcome of which lasts for years. Regulation as inspection provides a snapshot, but not a moving picture. Regulation in the health sector doesn't prevent failure, just as our current Ofsted approach doesn't, but it does alert us to where failure exists. It might be that an institution doesn't know it's failing, and in a few cases, tries to ignore that it might be, and in the worst cases tries to cover it up. Independent scrutiny has been established in this country to separate the Government from public sector bodies, but is this really the right approach? Some will say it is essential that Ofsted inspects schools independently from politics. However, if the role of Ofsted is school improvement and if the role of Government is school improvement, why the distance?

When the first CQC framework was established, it was fairly crude and judged an institution to be either compliant or not compliant. If it was not compliant then there may have been some minor changes to make, or if there were major issues then there would have been some enforcement activity and then regular monitoring. This is not too different from if a school is judged to be unsatisfactory now. The CQC then moved to awarding star ratings, but this was abandoned as it didn't seem appropriate to award stars to such complex institutions.

After a meeting of ministers it was decided that the CQC would adopt the grading approach used by Ofsted. When big, graded inspections started huge teams of people, each team with expertise in different areas, would go into hospitals, clipboards in hands, and inspect provision. These teams were made up of current practitioners, advisory inspectors and other stakeholders with lived experiences. I was told that for an early inspection of Barts Hospital in London eighty people arrived in coaches to conduct the process. Although not repeated it does show what would be needed if experts really did inspect their own specialisms. In school inspections, as I previously described, I have never understood how I, nor an inspector, could really make a secure judgement of learning in a classroom where I or they were not a subject or phase specialist. The nuances are too great. I can make generalisations, and good ones, but I am not an expert in every subject discipline or aspect of school life.

CHAPTER 8
MOVING FORWARD WITH A SELF-IMPROVING SYSTEM AND SYSTEM LEADERSHIP

Some of us will remember the Every Child Matters (ECM) agenda from 2003, and the Every School a Great School slogan. The ECM agenda had five themes which I remember trying to memorise as SHEEP: stay safe, be healthy, enjoy and achieve, make a positive contribution and achieve economic well-being. Ofsted inspectors would actually quiz you on these, and my headteacher at the time had a poster made for her wall and stuck it up in front of her desk so she could also quiz us each time we came into her office, to check we wouldn't get caught out if asked. The five themes required multi-agency teams to work together and really did place the child at the centre of the government's work to ensure every child could achieve these goals. I would happily have schools held to account over their efforts towards these.

'Every school a great school' became a popular phrase later that decade. There was much work being done around system leadership, such as that of David Hopkins, and many local authorities and early federations of schools had this as a key heading in their strategy papers. What I took from this at the time was that schools would work together to improve all schools for every child. I still believe in the possibility that parents could send their children to their local school, if they wanted to, knowing that all schools were good. I was fortunate enough to be involved in the London Challenge initiative (2003-2011) which led on some of this system leadership work to improve London schools. The key objectives of the London Challenge initiative were:

- To raise standards in the poorest performing schools.
- To narrow the attainment gap between pupils in London.
- To create more 'good' and 'outstanding' schools.

In 2006, Ofsted reported that between 2001 and 2005 the work of London Challenge had contributed to improved GCSE outcomes in London schools, an improvement faster than in England overall. In 2010 Ofsted reported that, 'London Challenge has continued to improve outcomes for pupils in London's primary and secondary schools at a faster rate than nationally. London's secondary schools continue to perform better than those in the rest of England.'[126] There are several studies which show it is hard to separate the achievements of this work from other local London factors, but there is definitely evidence to show that this initiative contributed to an increase in standards. The reason I mention this now is because of the power of this type of work; a self-improving school system where leaders work with each other, not in competition, where good practice is shared honestly and where leaderS work across systems, freely sharing their expertise and lessons learned and ensuring strategies are appropriate for individual context, not a one size fits all approach to school improvement.

Working together, improving every school and focusing on every child will drive school improvement much more than the regulations and inspection framework we currently have. The question is, how do we get both inspection and regulation to ensure schools are effective and young people are safe? At the same time, we need confidence that system leadership and the self-improving system will return greater gains in school improvement, benefitting all children and society as a whole.

In a series of conceptual pieces about school-to-school relationships and school improvement in England, David Hargreaves argued that 'clusters of schools working in partnership could potentially create a

---

126 Ofsted (2010) *London Challenge*. Available at: https://dera.ioe.ac.uk/2143/1/London%20Challenge.pdf

self-improving school system' and that the notion was supported by the government of the day. He goes on to note that, 'inter-school partnerships are flourishing in many different forms across thousands of schools in England in response to the coalition government's policy of transferring the main responsibility for teacher development and school improvement away from local authorities and other providers and directly to schools themselves.'[127]

The 2018 NFER report *What Impact Does Accountability Have On Curriculum, Standards and Engagement In Education?* references a 2011 NCSL study[128] focusing on disadvantaged pupils:

> *There are suggestions that primary and secondary schools that were supported by the initiative of 'National Support Schools (NSSs)' contributed to the closing of an attainment gap between pupils eligible for free school meals (FSM) and those who were not. This study reports that the schools which were 'supported by an NSS for more than one year showed that the attainment of pupils eligible for FSM in these supported schools improved at a faster rate than national averages between 2008 and 2010'.[129]*

This drive saw much school-to-school support across the country. National Leaders of Education, Specialist Leaders of Education and the outreach work of National Teaching Schools all contributed to this self-improving system, with encouraging results seen across schools.

There were great strengths and great gains during this period, but I feel a huge amount of this momentum has been lost and we have returned to an 'Ofsted knows best' model with a de-professionalisation of education as a body of knowledgeable people working together for system reform. This stagnation has meant that we did not get as far as we could have

---

127 Hargreaves, D. H. (2012) *A self-improving school system: towards maturity.* Nottingham: NCSL. Available at: https://dera.ioe.ac.uk/15804/1/a-self-improving-school-system-towards-maturity.pdf

128 NCSL (2011) *System leadership: does school-to-school-support close the gap?* Nottingham: NCSL. Available at: https://www.gov.uk/government/publications/system-leadership-does-school-to-school-support-close-the-gap

129 NFER (2018) *What Impact Does Accountability Have On Curriculum, Standards and Engagement In Education? A Literature Review.* Available at: https://www.nfer.ac.uk/media/3032/nfer_accountability_literature_review_2018.pdf

done in the ambition of Every School a Great School with all schools being sustainably managed and self-monitored and supported. In a model presented by David Hopkins (figure 33) we were in the process of moving from a period of great prescription to a self-improving system. We could go back to this model, but the nature of differing multi-academy trusts takes away this single movement and means we have fragmentation in the system, with some schools simply being left out altogether.

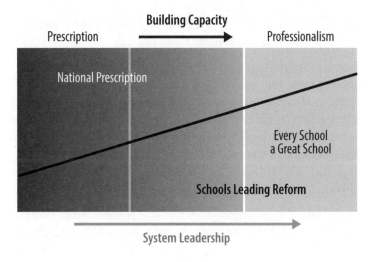

Figure 33. Towards system-wide sustainable reform[130]

Of course, this utopia may be hard to achieve but there was some great work being done through the Teaching Schools, London and City Challenge, the continuing work of Challenge Partners, and the School Partnership Programme. This is why system leadership as the main driver of such an approach is so important. System leaders care about, and work for, the success of other schools as well as their own. They measure their success in terms of improving all the schools they work with and not just their own, or those within their MAT. It is difficult to imagine the move across from prescription to professionalism happening within our current

---

130 Hopkins, D. (2022) *School Improvement: Precedents and Prospects.* East Melbourne: CSE. Available at: https://humelausanne.ch/wp-content/uploads/2022/09/CSE-Leading-Education-Series12-1.pdf

political system, which is a reason why I believe education needs to be taken out of politics: it will give us a chance to make a long-term strategic plan for educational improvement, as suggested by so many.

In terms of inspecting schools, I outline my manifesto in the final chapter of this book, but this self-improving system also offers the opportunity for peer review, for networking and collaboration where schools can support each other in a meaningful way, with no contradiction between collaboration, support and competition. Where leaders are concerned about standards, the quality and changing landscape of pedagogy, and equity, so that every child matters and every community matters.

SELF-IMPROVING SYSTEM AND PEER REVIEWS

Last year, the Accountability Commission reported that the way in which schools were being held to account for standards was doing more harm than good. In our report, Improving School Accountability, we concluded that to unleash potential across the country we need to rebalance holding schools to account with helping them to improve.[131]

This NAHT report *The Principles of Effective School-to-School Peer Review* continues 'Peer review was identified by the Commission as a potentially positive way in which schools could help one another to improve' and recognises that too few schools are involved in this type of activity. The report suggests that, 'To become a fully self-led system, where teachers and school leaders are able to exercise their professional capabilities towards a common goal of improving the life chances of all young people, we believe peer review and collaborative working must be the norm, not an exception.'

The report recognises that evidence exists to prove that schools working together can lead to overall improvements in the system, and this form of 'lateral accountability means that school performance becomes part of a system-level professional expectation, enabling a culture of continuous improvement and shared responsibility for outcomes across schools'.

---

131 NAHT (2019) *The Principles of Effective School-to-School Peer Review.* Available at: https://www.naht.org.uk/Portals/0/PDF's/NAHT%20Peer%20Review%20 Report%20(new).pdf?ver=2021-05-23-113106-710

The report sets out 16 key principles for effective peer review which are summarised in figure 34.

WHAT PEER REVIEW IS	WHAT PEER REVIEW ISN'T
A focus on improvement	A focus on proving
Based on an agreed framework	A mock inspection
Reciprocal and inclusive – for all schools wherever they are on their improvement journey	Strong schools reviewing 'weaker' schools
Underpinned by a coaching approach, done in a culture of enquiry, learning and growth	Giving advice or being judgmental
Focused, planned with feedback based on evidence and the analysis of data	A 'learning walk'
Peer review leads to a written or verbal summary collaboratively agreed between the reviewer/s and the host school	Concluded with a report written by an external reviewer in isolation

Figure 34. NAHT principles of peer review

The report finishes with a few points about what peer review is not. One of these reads: 'It's not about top-down accountability, performance management or trying to catch you out, but is about the horizontal accountability and support which peer practitioners can provide for each other with the best interest of pupils at heart.' I have every confidence that we have the power and the capacity and the will in our education system to move towards this type of school improvement journey.[132]

In *Peer review: a better alternative to Ofsted?* Kate Chhatwal writes that, 'Ofsted's "guiding principle" is to be a "force for improvement through intelligent, responsible and focused inspection and regulation." Yet last year's National Audit Office report revealed that less than half of headteachers felt that their latest inspection led to any improvement. That's because our formal accountability system is geared more to shaming than support, competition than collaboration, intervention than improvement. Look elsewhere and you will find that peer review and mutual accountability is a greater driver of school improvement than any top-down scrutiny.' She goes on to say, 'It's an accountability provided by the commitment we make to our children, parents and communities, and

132 Ibid.

to each other as fellow educators. The commitment to a relentless pursuit of excellence through mutual support and challenge.'

Referencing her work with Challenge Partners she describes four ways to make peer review 'a really strong tool for accountability and improvement':

Independence

Reviews should be led by someone with no vested interest beyond ensuring the rigour and integrity of the process, and especially that it is improvement-focused. The review team they lead should be constituted of peer leaders with the geographical, emotional and mental distance to give a truly honest appraisal of how the school or MAT is doing.

Review with the school

The second point – and one which really distinguishes it from an inspection – is that it must be done with, not to, the school or MAT being reviewed. This means making the school's leaders part of the review team, inviting them to interrogate what is going on in their own institution alongside the external reviewers. Doing so generates a rich professional dialogue in which pairs of leaders who have seen the same lessons and books, spoken together to middle leaders and so on, can reflect and conclude together about the strengths and areas for improvement in what they've seen.

Skeletons in the cupboards

A third feature of peer review that makes it both effective and different to an Ofsted visit is that it invites the host to open doors that would remain closed during an inspection. Peer review is an opportunity to fling open the closets and raise the carpets on the things that aren't going so well, on the "wicked" issues where additional eyes and expertise can help the leaders to see more clearly and find a way forward. For many, this is the hardest, but also most valuable, aspect of peer review. It takes courage to expose those skeletons, but it is also how the best insights and most productive discussions take place.

A commitment to better outcomes

The final feature (and prerequisite for such soul-baring) is the trust that comes from adherence to commonly-held values and a commitment to securing better outcomes in all schools and MATs, not just one's own. The pledge of each review team is to leave the school or MAT in a better state than they found it by contributing to the institution's understanding of its strengths (which they are encouraged to share), and what and how it can improve.

Our schools and MATs commit to work together before and after their annual reviews to share their experience and expertise, so peer review becomes a comma in an ongoing professional dialogue about how collectively to make all our schools better. It is this, as much as the review, that gives peer accountability its power, because it is about a responsibility we all share, not just to the children and communities we serve directly, but to each other.[133]

Another peer review approach is the Education Development Trust's (EDT) *Schools Partnership Programme*, reviewed in 2023 by the Education Endowment Foundation (EEF). The key features of this programme are:

- *This is based around partnerships of 3 – 7 schools working through a three part programme involving: self review; peer review; and follow up school-to-school support.*

- *Schools are trained in how to effectively undertake a continuous cycle of self review, peer reviews and follow up school-to-school support. Senior and middle leaders are the key participants, and each cluster nominates "Improvement Champions" who receive extra support to develop their facilitation skills and evidence-based approaches to school improvement.[134]*

This looks like the perfect improvement cycle: design strategic self-review activities in your own school to identify school priorities, then use the

---

133 Chhatwal, K. (2019) Peer review: a better alternative to Ofsted? *TES Magazine*. 5 February. Available at: https://www.tes.com/magazine/archive/peer-review-better-alternative-ofsted

134 EEF (2023) *Schools Partnership Programme. Education Development Trust*. Available at: https://educationendowmentfoundation.org.uk/projects-and-evaluation/projects/schools-partnership-programme-spp

peer review model to work with a group of schools to help you clarify this improvement agenda or identify other areas to improve and then work with these partners to add capacity into the areas needing support.

The programme itself came about because:

> *The need for lateral school-to school partnerships has become apparent in the face of evidence that neither top-down centrally imposed change, nor pure competition can achieve sustained improvement across school systems (Burns and Koster, 2016). The aim, rather, has been to "unleash greatness" by asking school system leaders to work together in ways which transfer knowledge, expertise, and capacity within and between schools, so that all schools improve, and all children achieve their potential' (DfE, 2010).*[135]

The 2023 evaluation of the SPP discussed this type of system-led work, and comments that an increase in peer review and evaluation activity which promotes self-accountability is 'a key step towards self-regulation, in which schools take greater ownership of their quality assurance, not only through self evaluation, but through exposing their work to the scrutiny and perceptions of trusted peers'.

The report sees school peer review as, 'a form of school internal evaluation and a supplement to the regional and national accountability system, in which formative evaluation and greater levels of professional accountability are emphasised compared with external forms of accountability such as inspections.'

Two key findings from the review of the SPP were that:

- School peer review is a popular approach to school improvement.
- The programme is intended to build capacity and capability across clusters of schools so they can gradually take more responsibility for their own development and maturity and lead their own improvement. Over time, local areas will own the SPP model, and continue to develop it so it has an impact locally.

---

135 EEF (2023) *Schools Partnership Programme: Evaluation Report.* London: EEF. Available at: https://d2tic4wvo1iusb.cloudfront.net/documents/projects/SPP-Evaluation-report.pdf?v=1682594246

The evaluators found many advantages to the programme, which they saw as really appreciating the local context of schools, a recurring theme in this book. They highlight the low stakes nature of peer review which, 'improves and openness between schools so issues can be freely discussed without them being written up in a publicly shared report.'

Other positive findings included:

- *At school level, the programme improved school leadership teams' self-reported abilities to identify their own strengths and weaknesses, to draw on expertise, and share partnership capacities.*

- *Surveys of reviewers learned valuable skills of reviewing and self-evaluation; and school leaders learned how to collaborate more rigorously and transparently, offering increasing challenges to each other with time, and enabling more fluid knowledge exchange and shared professional development that benefited their staff and schools.*

- *A range of positive teacher-reported outcomes.*

- *Participants perceived the programme to have been helpful in developing stronger partnerships, increasing levels of trust, sharing and transparency, and clearer structures to work towards shared improvement objectives. These self reported benefits were more likely to be found in schools with pupils that had higher levels of deprivation and these benefits were perceived as significantly greater in the SPP schools than matched schools.*[136]

David Godfrey has been working on school peer review models for some time but still finds that, 'despite the increased use of school peer review in system reform and school improvement, very little research has been conducted on this model and there is a dearth of literature that looks at the phenomenon internationally.'[137] His work led me to a paper *Toward a model of school inspections in a polycentric system* in which Frans Janssens and Melanie Ehren outline an alternative approach to inspection which is less of a vertical hierarchical model and one which is again more systems driven. The paper outlines a polycentric approach to school evaluation

---

136 Ibid.
137 Godfrey, D. (2020) *School Peer Review for Educational Improvement and Accountability.* New York: Springer.

and shares some examples of 'newer inspection models to evaluate the effectiveness of a range of different networks'. Such models for evaluating the effectiveness of networks could be used alongside a peer review and improvement model to ensure it was working. The paper finds that by employing a network of partners who work together towards school evaluation and improvement, trust and openness grows and improvement is more widespread. It goes on to demonstrate, 'how Inspectorates of Education can develop a set of intelligent and more flexible evaluation models and intervention strategies that would improve the performance of the entire education system by purposefully providing relevant actors with feedback, to improve relations in the networks and increase openness to external stakeholders and information.'[138]

The London challenge initiative was a school improvement programme launched in 2003. It was initially set up to support London secondary schools but did some work with primaries and was extended out as City Challenge across the country. Schools that were identified as needing the most help were called 'Keys to Success Schools' and advisers were attached to each of these schools to provide support. The advisers worked with a range of other supportive partners such as NLEs and SIPs to develop intervention programmes. A strong feature of this programme was the school-to-school peer support approach, maybe because schools were not seen as failing but given 'keys to success', maybe because of the strong support targeted at schools who needed it and the capacity of this strong team working together. Partly because of the strength and depth of this peer support, London Challenge was seen at the time to have a remarkable impact in improving London schools.

There is a lot of good to say about peer review, and much evidence to suggest it works in terms of helping schools improve. It takes away the labelling of Ofsted and when working with their peers, schools are not left to get on with the suggestions themselves but are supported to do so. Schools do need to be held to account, but what if the improvement agenda and activity was left to them?

---

138 Janssens, F. and Ehren, M. (2016) Toward a model of school inspections in a polycentric system. *Evaluation and Program Planning*, (56), 88-98. Available at: http://www.schoolinspections.eu/wp-content/uploads/2017/02/Janssens-en-Ehren.pdf

CHAPTER 9
PROPOSALS FOR NEW SCHOOL ACCOUNTABILITY MODELS

When I decided to write this book, I thought this chapter would be the hardest to tackle. Naturally I already had a perception of Ofsted stemming from my own experiences and previous work on school accountability, and I probably had some ideas about what should, or could, be done differently. I was prepared for these preconceived notions to be robustly challenged during my research, and on some level I probably thought I would encounter opposing, deeply entrenched, politicised, emotional, and even argumentative views about Ofsted and the future of school accountability. However, while it is a contentious and emotive subject, what I found for the most part in my many hours of reading, listening, research and reflection, was a general consensus that while changes and improvements are urgently required, there is an agreement from all quarters that the most important end point of any inspection or accountability system must be that it improves opportunities and outcomes for all our young people.

My thinking on the subject can be distilled as follows:

- Remove the overall grade.
- Schools should go back to writing their own SEF.
- Inspectors should visit to look at the SEF and might say if a school is 'effective' or 'ineffective' (though I'm still not sure even about this language).
- LAs should inspect safeguarding annually.

- Peer review will help schools improve through a school-led self-improving system.
- An accountability framework written by a range of relevant experts.

Obviously it's much more complex than this and all these suggestions need to be thought through, but I think this sums it up.

I had another word with ChatGPT AI which had its own ideas when asked 'What could be an alternative model to Ofsted?'

> One alternative model to Ofsted could be a peer review system, where teachers and school leaders review and evaluate each other's performance. This could help create a more collaborative and supportive culture within schools, and allow for more nuanced evaluations of teaching quality. Another alternative could be a system where schools are evaluated by a panel of experts in education, rather than by a single inspector. This could help ensure that evaluations are more objective and based on a wider range of perspectives.

It is interesting to see that the sources available to ChatGPT mirror the sources I have collated in writing this book, in that they describe a more sensible approach to monitoring and suggest a model of accountability that really is about school improvement.

A move from a vertical to a more horizontal accountability model would be welcomed by many. As we have learned from such models in other countries, we can combine accountability from the top insofar as schools do need to be held accountable, but in a much-reduced form. We could demonstrate we value the professionalism and expertise in our school system and use peer review as the vehicle that collects the evidence to identify strengths and areas to improve, and we need the support system to help all schools to act on their improvement agendas, not just those in MATs.

WHAT THE UNIONS SAY

'It is right that, as a publicly funded universal service, the education system should be subject to an appropriate, constructive and proportionate system of accountability'.[139] In their *School Accountability Position Statement*, the NASUWT note that, 'Across the UK, hierarchical accountability is the dominant form of school accountability. For example, governments/ administrations use inspection, test and examination data, and in England, published performance tables to hold schools to account. The hierarchical approach that dominates external systems of accountability is often replicated through accountability systems that operate within individual schools, such as the performance management of teachers.' They believe that there are ten principles which should underpin our approach to accountability in schools:

Systems of school accountability should:

Trust teachers as professionals

Systems of accountability must not be designed to operate in ways that could undermine teachers' professional status, integrity or commitment. Accountability systems should also recognise that, as professionals, teachers have particular expertise which means that they may be best placed to make judgements about the quality and effectiveness of particular aspects of education.

Support schools to provide a curriculum that is broad, balanced and meets the needs of all learners

Accountability systems should value the range of ways in which schools help learners to engage in learning, progress and achieve. Teachers should be actively engaged in decisions about the design and implementation of curricula and assessment and the related accountability arrangements.

Support schools to maintain high educational standards

Accountability judgements should be holistic. Teachers and school leaders should contribute to decisions about improving the quality of provision for pupils.

---

139 NASUWT (2023) *Inspection and Accountability.* Available at: https://www.nasuwt. org.uk/advice/in-the-classroom/inspection-and-accountability.html

Support teachers and school leaders to improve the quality of teaching and learning

Accountability arrangements should complement efforts to improve progress and outcomes of pupils. Teachers and school leaders should have an entitlement to high-quality CPD and time within the working day to access such CPD. Accountability should recognise teachers' professional knowledge and expertise rather than focus on penalising teachers.

Encourage and support teachers and school leaders to work co-operatively and collaboratively

Teachers should be encouraged to work together to develop and share effective practice. Collaborative working, within and beyond the school, should be recognised as an important form of CPD.

Be fair and equitable

Teachers should not be penalised because, for example, they are inclusive or work with learners who have challenging or complex needs. Furthermore, teachers should not be penalised because they do not teach a 'core' subject.

Ensure that teachers and school leaders are supported to engage in dialogue and collaborative decision-making

The collective voice of teachers should be recognised as of critical importance when forming judgements about the quality and effectiveness of education provision.

Ensure that the needs and priorities of learners and parents are considered and taken into account appropriately in decision-making

'Pupil voice' should not be used in ways which undermine the professional status, integrity or judgements of teachers and school leaders.

Be streamlined and avoid unnecessary bureaucracy and workload

Accountability systems should not place unnecessary or excessive workload and bureaucratic burdens on teachers and school leaders.

> **Be rigorous, reasonable and valid**
>
> *The public and the teaching profession should have confidence in the judgements made. Inspection and accountability systems respect the professionalism of teachers, do not impose excessive and unnecessary workload burdens, and provide genuine support to the work of schools in raising standards and promoting educational achievement.*[140]

Let's take from here the principle that teachers and leaders be treated as professionals, and their knowledge and expertise recognised and valued. Let's also take that school leaders should work collaboratively to improve standards beyond their own school, for all children.

Reporting on the 2023 ASCL discussion paper *The Future of Inspection*, Sally Wheale, writing in *The Guardian*, says the discussion paper, 'accepts there should be an independent inspectorate, but says Ofsted is losing the trust of the profession. It suggests the current grading system, which can stigmatise schools that receive negative judgments, should be replaced with a narrative description of strengths and weaknesses … ASCL's general secretary, Geoff Barton, said: "Graded judgments are a woefully blunt tool with which to measure performance, failing to account for the different circumstances under which schools operate. Negative judgments come with huge stigma attached and create a vicious circle that makes improvement more difficult."'

In their discussion paper ASCL also set out their principles for future inspection:

- Inspection should be constructive, not punitive.
- Inspection activity should be based on professional dialogue.
- Inspection outcomes must be reliable and valid in order to carry the trust of the profession and other stakeholders.
- Inspection frameworks, and their implementation, must be transparent.
- Significant changes to inspection should only be introduced following a thorough pilot and a detailed impact analysis.

---

140 Ibid.

There isn't much new here but the paper does call for some significant changes to the current inspection model:

1. Removal of overall graded judgements.
2. Notice of inspection.
3. Transparency over inspection activity.
4. A review into how pupil voice is considered during inspection.

They also call for new Ofsted Standards and suggest that Ofsted should publish its inspector training material and update the inspection handbook and reporting to better reflect the role of trusts in school effectiveness. In future inspection models they want to see the 'national curriculum as the only document which sets out the government's curriculum requirements or expectations', and they want Ofsted to, 'produce separate handbooks, frameworks and standards for different phases, and require lead inspectors to have relevant leadership experience of the phase they are inspecting.' As well as removing 'safeguarding and health and safety from the inspection standards, replacing them with a light-touch annual audit.'[141]

So, remove grades, have simpler, phase-specific frameworks, end no-notice inspections and introduce annual safeguarding audits.

In the paper *A Great Education for Every Child* (2021) ASCL also call for schools and colleges to be part of, 'strong, supportive partnerships, in which every institution is both a "giver" and a "taker" ... where staff will work ... collaboratively, and actively seek ways to share knowledge, expertise and resources. They are a key mechanism for supporting struggling schools to improve, and for the development and dissemination of high quality teaching and learning. They consider themselves collectively responsible for all the children and young people in the partnership, and work closely with other local education providers to ensure a joined up approach across a local area.' With 'clarity and consistency around the role of different bodies, particularly "middle tier" organisations such as local authorities and Regional Schools Commissioners. System governance, as well as the governance of individual schools, colleges and trusts, is strong.'

---

141 ASCL (2023) *The Future of Inspection.* Available at: https://www.ascl.org.uk/ASCL/media/ASCL/Our%20view/Campaigns/The-future-of-inspection-an-ASCL-discussion-paper.pdf

Sounds very much like a system-led approach to school improvement! In terms of accountability the report outlines that, 'Schools and colleges are held to account in a proportionate, intelligent, supportive way. The accountability system recognises the different contexts in which different schools and colleges operate, and seeks to minimise potentially distorting effects or unintended consequences. It actively encourages organisations to work collaboratively for the good of all children and young people in a local area. Schools are held to account against the national curriculum, and against a slim and intelligent set of nationally agreed measures which go beyond academic performance. There is also capacity for individual schools or colleges, or groups of schools and colleges, to determine additional measures against which they want to hold themselves to account.' There is recognition here of context and encouragement for all schools to be equally involved. It will be interesting to see if the 'nationally agreed measures' of accountability take shape and to see the full range of stakeholders represented in this discussion.

Recommendations from the NAHT were drawn up in *Improving School Accountability*. Their key proposals for inspection include:

- A new role for Ofsted, focused on identifying failure and providing stronger diagnostic insight for schools that are struggling.
- The 'outstanding' judgement should be replaced with a more robust system for identifying specific excellence within the sector, to increase the take-up of highly effective, evidence-based practice.
- Ofsted should commission research to determine the format and nature of inspection required, in order to provide reliable judgements and reciprocal benefits for schools.

They recognise that Ofsted has a role in identifying school failure, but that the inspectorate should provide, 'a clearer, more detailed diagnostic analysis of the issues that have resulted in a school being judged as "requires improvement"'. They believe that, 'Ofsted should continue to have a role in supporting the ambition that all schools are good schools … and it should do this by checking that no school is failing or at risk of decline; checking that standards aren't slipping; investigating the extent to which the school is outward looking and collaborative; and rooting out sharp practices and gaming, including off-rolling.' Rather than Ofsted continuing to provide research papers, the NAHT 'believes there are other actors better placed to identify excellence in the system, in order to unleash the potential of the school-led system'. Like others they support 'incentivising collaborative working and peer support' and they recognise the benefits of peer reviews as, 'a good demonstration of the profession stepping up to take responsibility for school improvement and accepting accountability to peers in their community.'

The Accountability Commission set down eight guiding principles for the development of a future accountability system:

1. *Judge schools on the impact they have, in helping to ensure that all pupils make the progress they should. An accountability system should help not hinder the provision of excellent education for all.*

2. *Be fair to all schools, irrespective of circumstance or context. Good teachers and leaders should be properly recognised for, and not dissuaded from, working in tough schools.*

3. *Accept the inherent limitations of data for accountability purposes and recognise high-quality, on the ground review as the most effective way to form a sound judgement of any school's effectiveness.*

4. *Identify signs of failure or decline early to reduce the extent of remedial action required to address issues and to ensure supportive challenge characterises interventions.*

5. *Encourage school leaders to take responsibility for their own school improvement and not limit ambition for what is possible.*

6. *Incentivise, encourage and value collective responsibility for pupil outcomes across schools regionally and nationally.*

7. *Be transparent and provide parents with easy to understand information, to improve the clarity of meaning while reducing any associated unintended consequences.*

8. *Reduce workload, relieve stress and dial down the anxiety associated with accountability for pupils, teachers and school leaders, recognising the duty to safeguard mental health and well-being.*[142]

---

142 NAHT (2018) *Improving School Accountability.* Available at: https://www.naht.org.uk/Portals/0/PDF's/Improving%20school%20accountability.pdf?ver=2021-04-27-121950-093/

The National Education Union (NEU) goes further than other unions, calling for Ofsted to be replaced entirely. Their call to sign a petition to replace Ofsted, set out in early 2023, is hard-hitting:

> *Ofsted has never published any research to prove that its inspections accurately reflect the quality of education schools provide. Comprehensive, independent analysis of Ofsted judgements show they discriminate against schools in deprived areas – awarding 'outstanding' grades to four times more secondary schools with better-off pupils than schools with students who are worse off. A major research study showed that, even when schools in deprived areas are making excellent value-added progress, they are still more likely to be given poor Ofsted judgements.*

> *Teachers and leaders know that working in disadvantaged areas is likely to be harmful to their careers because of the unfairness of Ofsted judgements. It is harder to recruit and retain teachers in these schools. Poor children, who most need qualified and experienced teachers if they are to fulfil their potential, are least likely to get them.*

> *School inspection must be fair. It should be supportive. It should not be, as too many Ofsted inspections are, punitive.*

> *The stress and unsustainable workload generated by Ofsted is a major factor in the appalling teacher retention rates that blight English education. Nearly 40 per cent of teachers leave the profession within ten years. No education system can improve while it haemorrhages school leaders and teachers.*

> *We must create a new approach to school and college evaluation which is effective and fair.*[143]

The NEU refers to findings from the OECD which they say offers 'nine features that should underpin an effective accountability framework with pupils at its centre'. None of these features are present in the current approach taken to school inspection in England.

---

143 NEU (2023) *Replace Ofsted. Let Teachers Teach.* Available at: https://actionnetwork. org/forms/replace-ofsted-let-teachers-teach?source=direct_link&

1. *Support and challenge the work of teachers and leaders and assist schools and colleges to support and improve their performance.*

2. *Encourage teacher creativity and local innovation and promote teacher self-efficacy and agency.*

3. *Be founded on a shared understanding of effective practices in teaching and recognise that this is the subject of ongoing research and discussion, can be highly contested and is open to interpretation and new developments.*

4. *Reflect the complexity of teachers' professional understanding and practice and not be driven by summative performance measures.*

5. *Support teaching quality by not increasing bureaucracy but making best use of sustainably generated information.*

6. *Be conducted by well-trained evaluators who are accountable for their contribution to quality education. The practice of any external evaluators must be monitored by consistent and effective quality assurance providers.*

7. *Support the development of schools and colleges as professional learning institutions with collegiate relations and professional dialogue between teachers and leaders.*

8. *Be compatible with well-aligned procedures for teacher recruitment, registration, induction and mentoring, support structures and professional instruments of evaluation.*

9. *Make connections between the different evaluation components to ensure that those components are sufficiently linked in order to avoid unnecessary bureaucracy, unhelpful duplication, and so that there are no conflicts between accountability processes.*[144]

The NEU is calling on the government to:

- Replace Ofsted with a school accountability system which is supportive, effective and fair.
- Work with teachers, leaders and other stakeholders to establish a commission to learn how school accountability is done in other high performing education nations.

---

144 NEU (2023) *Replacing Ofsted*. Available at: https://www.replaceofsted. valueeducation.org.uk/replacing-ofsted

- Develop an accountability system which commands the trust and confidence of education staff as well as parents and voters.

The details of what they hope to replace Ofsted with have not been set out in detail, rather this is billed as an opportunity for a range of stakeholders to work together to design a new accountability system.[145]

OTHER VOICES

The Labour Party has also set out its proposals for changes to the inspection regime in England. It calls for a 'national review of Ofsted to ensure that "the inspection and accountability regime makes the most positive and constructive contribution possible to the education system as a whole".'[146]

In a debate in Westminster in June 2022, Conservative MP Julian Sturdy talked about the accountability of Ofsted and said, 'there should be some humility on the part of Ofsted to recognise the fact that what its inspectors see during an inspection is, in the words of one of the respondents to the survey, "a snapshot in time", with the outcome of the inspection not always capturing the reality of the school.'

Stephen Morgan (Labour) added, 'School inspection must be a crucial part of our education system to deliver the best for our children, but I fear that the framework drives a tick-box culture, as echoed by other Members in the debate. It does not necessarily encourage the delivery of excellent education to every child. It also contributes to a growing recruitment and retention crisis in the teaching profession, which will inevitably have an impact in the classroom.' He went on to share Labour's plans: 'First, we would free up inspectors to work more closely with schools requiring improvement. They would be empowered to put in place plans to deliver sustained change in struggling schools, similar to the peer-to-peer support that worked so well in the London challenge. We would connect teachers and leaders with the training they need. Next, we would require Ofsted to report on a school's performance relative to other schools in its family,

---

145 NEU (2023) *Replace Ofsted. Let Teachers Teach.* Available at: https://actionnetwork. org/forms/replace-ofsted-let-teachers-teach?source=direct_link&

146 Booth, S. (2022) Major Labour review wants creative curriculum and less exams focus. *Schools Week.* 26 October. Available at: https://schoolsweek.co.uk/major-labour-review-calls-for-creative-curriculum-and-less-exams-focus/

or those with similar characteristics. That would recognise the short and long-term improvements that teachers plan, helping parents understand inspection results more clearly. We would also require Ofsted to report on areas of excellence within a school, so that we can celebrate what is great as well as what needs improvement. Working with school leaders and staff, we can reset the adversarial culture and refocus on the delivery of excellence for every child.'[147]

In 2021, Headteachers Roundtable wrote *An Alternative Education White Paper*, with its call for, 'a reform of Ofsted so that it can contribute constructively to the rebuilding process.' After the pandemic. The policy suggestions of the paper are set out below:

1. *Remove Ofsted grading – OFSTED inspection to be reformed with labelling and categorisation of schools and academies removed. The purpose of inspection should instead be to identify excellence, the capacity of an institution to assist in system-wide improvement, and the identification of areas requiring attention and support.*

2. *Contextualise school accountability – Inspection frameworks need to be fit for purpose and properly reflect the education sector that they are inspecting. Accountability judgements need to be informed by a full appreciation of a school's unique circumstances and contextual challenges, including levels of disadvantage.*

3. *Create a Headteacher recruitment and retention strategy – All school leaders, including Headteachers, Executive Headteachers and CEOs, should have access to regular professional supervision and all new Headteachers should be provided with an experienced mentor and a programme of high-quality professional development.*

4. *Reframe the education accountability system – A commission should be established, involving all Headteacher organisations, to establish an enquiry and review into the support, management, protection, and accountability that surrounds Headteachers and make recommendations to achieve a more coherent and purposeful accountability system.*

---

147 Hansard HC Deb vol. 715 col. 358-377 (8 June 2022) Available at: https://hansard. parliament.uk/commons/2022-06-08/debates/9D29510E-1454-4117-82AA-7B3B9911B1A2/OfstedAccountability

5. *Introduce specialist safeguarding audits – Establish a national safeguarding service to oversee an annual safeguarding audit for all schools and colleges. This annual audit should be conducted on a similar basis to financial audit, with RAG rating against a set of criteria and specific recommended actions.*[148]

The 2022 Times Education Commission report *Bringing Out The Best*, calls for, 'a reformed Ofsted that works collaboratively with schools to secure sustained improvement, rather than operating through fear, and a new "school report card" with a wider range of metrics including wellbeing, school culture, inclusion and attendance to unleash the potential of schools.' The report suggests that, 'reform is needed to make Ofsted feel less like a "big stick" and more of a "helping hand" and schools should get a "report card". There is no reason that Ofsted inspections should not be planned in advance.'[149]

Some former HMIs suggest having a specialist safeguarding inspector: 'It is time to deploy an inspector of safeguarding on a fairly regular basis to each school with the task of determining whether current arrangements appear safe and the school culture is positive.' They also suggest, 'it is time to reintroduce a requirement for all schools to complete a pithy self-evaluation statement that includes the views of parents and pupils and the findings of any peer reviews undertaken within the past year.' The group of former inspectors agree, 'we do not believe Ofsted should be disbanded but we do feel it needs to focus more sharply on the most important aspects and provide a vehicle for schools to share their own evaluations of their effectiveness.'[150]

---

148 Headteachers' Roundtable (2021) *An Alternative Education White Paper.* Available at: https://headteachersroundtable.files.wordpress.com/2021/07/headteachers-roundtable-alternative-white-paper-2021-final.pdf

149 Times Education Commission (2022) *Bringing Out The Best.* Available at: https://s3.documentcloud.org/documents/22056664/times-education-commission-final-report.pdf

150 Johnson, S., Price-Grimshaw, J., Lyons, A., Brown, D., Norris, F. and Williams, M. (2022) Former HMIs: Why Ofsted needs to change its priorities. *TES.* 19 October. Available at: https://www.tes.com/magazine/analysis/general/former-hmis-why-ofsted-needs-change-its-priorities?amp

TWITTER

One suggestion on Twitter was a report card. Former teacher and senior leader Daren White designed the one shown in figure 35 and kindly sent it to me. He explained, 'This dashboard overview is something I feel very strongly about having been through in excess of 20 inspections myself as a teacher and senior leader. My thinking behind this approach to school improvement reform was this; create a school improvement system where peer principals support each other for the benefit of all young people, regardless of which school roll they are on or where they live. This system would remove overall gradings completely, dispense with league tables and provide stakeholders with a balanced overview of strengths, priorities and journeys of improvement. The inspiration came from the CQC dashboards used with hospitals where, for example, my local hospital has considerable issues with regards to the A&E department, but the Burns Unit is sector leading. Knowing this information affords me a more informed opinion. I might be concerned if the hospital was "failing" and that's all I knew, but knowing there are pockets of excellence and improvement instils some confidence. The concept in the example is that a school is visited by a peer principal partner, an open and honest, non-pejorative review is conducted, not necessarily all in one or two days but over a period of visits giving a potentially fairer overview and the findings are agreed between the two principals, as are the recommended actions. The principal of the "reviewed school" then has the ongoing support of the peer principal moving forwards.'

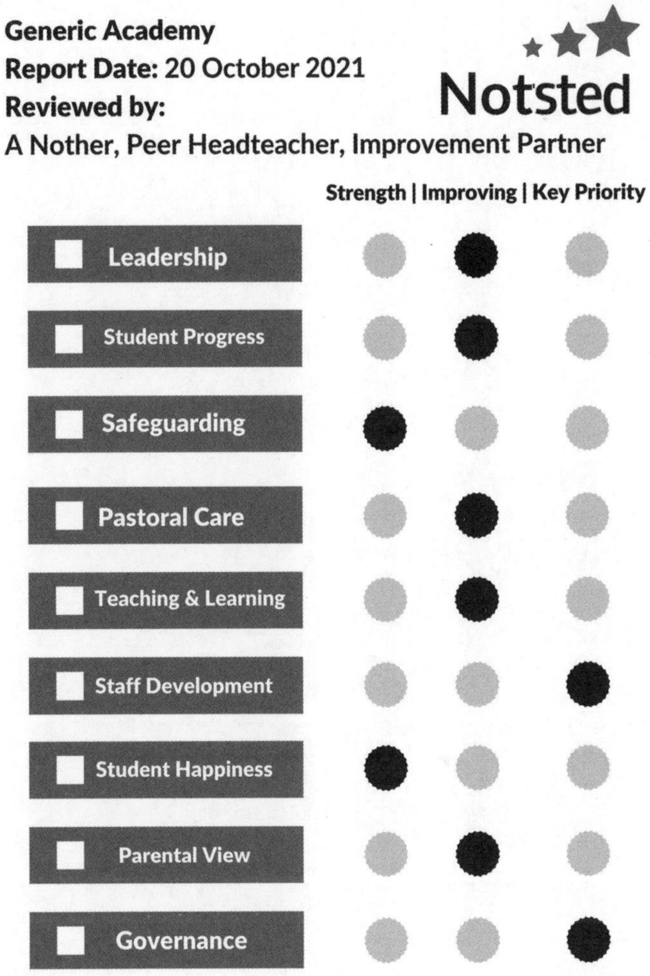
Generic Academy
Report Date: 20 October 2021
Reviewed by:
A Nother, Peer Headteacher, Improvement Partner
Notsted
Strength | Improving | Key Priority
Leadership
Student Progress
Safeguarding
Pastoral Care
Teaching & Learning
Staff Development
Student Happiness
Parental View
Governance

Figure 35. Darren White's report card

CHAPTER 10
RETHINKING INSPECTION

What if our approach to inspection was to use a truly strategic review model? We would start from a position of knowing that not everything will be great all the time, and that at times some things will be decidedly poor. We would encourage system-led practices to support schools with their own self-evaluation, using peer reviews to identify strengths and areas to improve in our schools. School Improvement Partners (SIPs) would call on Regional Education Advisors (REAs) to broker appropriate support. Without high stakes accountability we could unleash the potential for more risk-taking and innovation, as in other industries. We would see much more sharing of practice as the competitive element would be reduced, as would the money spent on banners on school fences. We would see ourselves moving towards a reality of 'all schools as great schools'. We would be held to account by experts looking at data in real time, triangulating outcomes, listening to stakeholder voices, looking at how robustly schools identify their own strengths and weaknesses; and the role of Ofsted and inspectors would be to shine a light on where improvements could be made, and galvanising support from where they knew complementary great practice existed. These professionals would come from the sector itself and all processes would be peer led.

We could use a model such as the one shown in figure 36 from Chapman and Sammons' *School self-evaluation for school improvement: what works and why?* which would give a structure but allow schools to drive the cycle relevant to their setting, which could be worked on with their SIPs and established peer partners. Schools would work out their own priorities and Ofsted would look at SEFs to evaluate how rigorous these priorities are, how robust the planned actions are, and what impacts are likely to be seen.

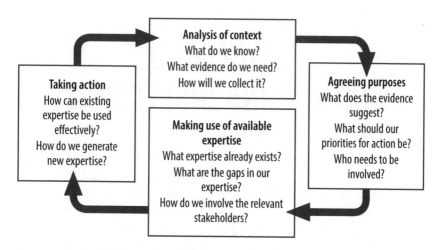

Figure 36. Towards context-specific school self-evaluation for school improvement[151]

This type of self-evaluation framework would be adapted by each school and would not only need to be 'sensitive to contextual and cultural diversity' but would 'also need to focus on developing the ability to facilitate meaningful conversations between those involved in the self-evaluation process, to generate and validate new knowledge and encourage participation to support the generation of trusting relationships between those involved.' inspection teams would then use the school's own SEF and identification of areas to improve to guide their inspection.[152]

The money saved from dispensing with the current inspection model could go directly into the school system, maybe through the REAs, to broker the required support, so the money actually makes a real impact, and is not just used for making a judgement on a report.

---

151 Chapman, C. and Sammons, P. (2013) *School self-evaluation for school improvement: what works and why?* Treading: CfBT. Available at: https://www.academia. edu/11341049/_School_self_evaluation_for_school_improvement_What_works_ and_why_?email_work_card=thumbnail

152 Ibid.

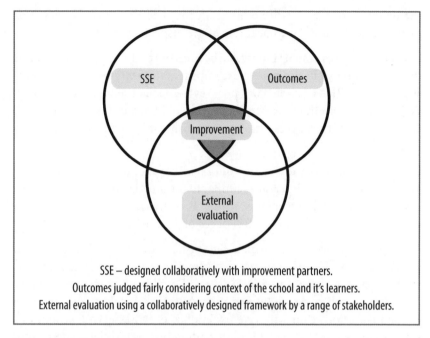

SSE – designed collaboratively with improvement partners.
Outcomes judged fairly considering context of the school and it's learners.
External evaluation using a collaboratively designed framework by a range of stakeholders.

Figure 37. A holistic approach to school improvement

I think we can combine a top-down inspection or accountability framework which judges a school to be effective or ineffective, and then horizontal relationships with partners who broker improvement opportunities, with regional educational advisors prioritising support for ineffective schools. Figure 37 demonstrates where this horizontal holistic approach would work together to lead to school improvement.

I am not suggesting a 'light touch' approach – there will be a framework which needs to be consulted on more widely with representatives from each of the teaching unions, research organisations such as the Education Endowment Foundation, the Teacher Development Trust, and teaching bodies such as the Chartered College for Teaching. This is essential to ensure statements about effective teaching are evidence based, not just aligned to current political thinking.

Safeguarding will be audited annually by the local authority using a joined-up assessment framework aligning with other children's services, the outcome of which will be listed on the school's own self-evaluation form which will form the backbone of the inspection itself.

The school improvement activity will be born out of the SEF, demonstrating the school knows itself, has robust impact statements and has brokered support from REAs. Schools will peer review each other and the outcomes will also feed into the SEF. The SEF itself will be word limited to mitigate against some of the adverse effects previously mentioned in support of its withdrawal.

During an inspection the team would use 'keeping in touch' meetings to give feedback to middle leaders (similar to the ones currently held between inspectors and senior staff) as so much of the helpful and productive discussion is lost when only a few pages of a report are written up.

Pupil performance data – which cannot be avoided – will be added as simply as possible with a focus on performance for particular groups of students such as DAS and SEND. The SEF will have space for a context statement which must be taken into account, and at least one member of the inspection team will have experience of working in a school in a similar context so that a real understanding of specific challenges can be recognised and acknowledged by the whole team.

Each school would have a registered school improvement partner (SIP), possibly delivered by the local authority, who would support the school in producing the SEF and liaising with the REAs.

Following an inspection, the REA, SIP and the school leadership team, would meet to review the inspection report, and review the SDP and SEF, adding any relevant actions or priorities, and the REA would then call on local support to assist with these.

A RETURN TO THE SELF-EVALUATION FORM (SEF)

So what if schools had to once again produce an annual SEF which was sent off to HMIs to interrogate? If there were unanswered lines of enquiry then Inspectors would arrange to visit the school, being explicit in advance as to what these themes were. The form would be online and word limited, avoiding some earlier criticisms of leaders writing lengthy tomes, and would force leaders to be much sharper with impact statements and not run into a full narrative of the work and life of the whole school. The form would have to be submitted by a certain date, like a tax return. Safeguarding might still be done by external bodies or local authorities who would in turn be inspected to ensure validity and rigour, and evidence of this audit would go on to the SEF. Similar audits already exist for finance, which is a genuine form of accountability as to how schools spend funds, especially in terms of holding state schools accountable for public funds.

If Ofsted really were a force for school improvement they could target which schools to visit and when. This approach would obviate the needs for grades, which as we have seen are unpopular with most groups discussed in this book, and a school would be deemed good or not yet good, effective or ineffective, although this language would never appear in public. It would be used to help target support, not publicly shame schools. If the Inspectorate finds 20% of schools to be ineffective then their limited resources would be directed towards these schools and REAs could be deployed appropriately to support these schools, leading to system-wide improvement for all!

A summary of these and other thoughts about rethinking inspection are shown in figure 38 below, I would also stop mocksteds and deep dives, which are not included in the table as I wouldn't replace them with anything!

Change	Replace with
Remove the grades.	No comments. Good – not yet good. Ofsted and REAs will focus support on schools not yet good.
Schools produce own versions of a SEF.	Schools fill in an online word-limited SEF showing evidence of: • annual safeguarding review • peer review activity • SIP involvement. Ofsted use these to evaluate how well schools know themselves and liaise with REAs to ensure support is going to the right places.
Peer reviews established.	These teams work not like an Ofsted team, but as real school improvement partners reviewing a school's own priorities. Challenge Partners or School Partnership Programme.

Ofsted don't judge safeguarding.	LAs carry out annual checks, also quality assured by Ofsted at intervals.
New framework.	Collaboration, consultation, views of all stakeholders including young people. Quality of education framework informed by educational research, for example the EEF, TDT, CCT, EBE, OECD, university work. Bringing together our increasing understanding of how children learn but also looking at what education is for and equipping students with skills for our changing world (similar to the Welsh curriculum).
Remove Ofsted engagement with research.	Leave this to the experts, but go back to producing case studies which are not to be slavishly followed but seen as just that.
Regular cycles of inspections.	Schools know which year and which term inspectors will come in. This means that partners working together will ensure the school is 'ready', and responsibilities shared.
The final report.	This is aimed at parents, showing a summary of the SEF and the inspection team's findings.
Lose the notion that 'one framework fits all'.	Produce different frameworks for the different sectors, co-produced with leaders from those sectors.
Inspections / frameworks are taken out of current educational policy thinking.	Educational thinking varies between educational leaders; this leads to changing priorities too often.
Complaints are not dealt with by Ofsted.	An independent complaints body is established.
Change inspections teams.	Ensure teams are made up of experts who have working knowledge of the sectors they are going into. Inspectors are also aware and take notice of a school's context. I would also consider employing a lay inspector: someone not involved in schools, but someone who has great knowledge about the local area and context, the needs of the communities, employment opportunities and so on.
Inspectors don't just see the SLT and chair of governors for KiT meetings and final feedback.	Inspectors give feedback to middle leaders through the visit so vital detail is not lost.

Figure 38. Changes to the current inspection model in England

There are many advantages of these suggested changes:

1. Re-Professionalisation of the system and teachers.
2. No game playing and staff are allowed to get on with their own (and by extension the school's) priorities.
3. The quality of education is informed by a range of research from England and internationally.
4. Annual SEFs are collaboratively constructed through peer-to-peer work, focus on a school's own priorities and employ SIPs who are in schools every half term working alongside leaders to support improvement planning.
5. The removal of grades eliminates the high-stakes nature of inspection.
6. Safeguarding – which is so important – is carried out much more regularly.
7. Pilot inspections are carried out, and, as now, would be a crucial part of the new framework process.
8. Much greater student involvement empowers students and gives them greater agency.
9. REAs add support, not just an additional layer of monitoring, by brokering support across the system and helping to put together the peer review teams.

When I spoke with Carl Smith, a school principal I quoted earlier in the book, he suggested a jury service approach to being on inspection teams. This would mean all school leaders had a certain amount of inspection training and that schools would be compensated financially by the treasury for when these leaders were out of school. It would be an expectation that this would happen and would alleviate the uneven playing field we have now, where some schools have Ofsted-trained leaders and some do not.

LAST WORDS

Obviously, all these thoughts and suggestions would need much greater examination and development, but a full review of our current inspection model must happen. A wide range of stakeholders need to be involved, research from effective inspection models from other countries needs to be looked at, and pilot work would need to be undertaken. It seems obvious, but the education system is so important to us all, and life changing for many. The fact that Ofsted takes time away from us focusing on what matters most in schools is, frankly, scandalous. We need a way that we can all work together, not at odds with each other. Children first, process second.

The conclusion is that surely there must be a better way. This book draws on a range of views to suggest new models of accountability that are about school improvement, and describes a common-sense approach, one that uses the experience and capacity in the existing school system. It offers a manifesto for systemic change in the English school inspection model that could provide genuine, long-lasting and significant benefits for students, teachers, parents/carers, schools and society as a whole.